Understanding
Understanding

Understanding
Understanding

PAUL ZIFF

Cornell University Press

ITHACA AND LONDON

First published 1972 by Cornell University Press.
Published in the United Kingdom by Cornell University Press Ltd., 2-4 Brook Street, London W1Y 1AA.

International Standard Book Number 0-8014-0744-3
Library of Congress Catalog Card Number 72-4573

Printed in the United States of America by Vail-Ballou Press, Inc.

Librarians: Library of Congress cataloging information appears on the last page of the book.

To my father and mother
William and Bessie Ziff

Preface

The essays of this volume were designed to be mutually informing, to yield a composite function with which to make a beginning, to begin a mapping of a peculiar domain. The fundamental problem is to understand how one understands what is said: that problem is insoluble at present. But my attempt is not of the impossible. Neither have I been concerned to put forth a continuous complete analysis of the topic: a show of continuity could only be fraudulent, a claim to completeness at best presumptuous nonsense. The attempt here is rather to delineate a relevant set of parameters worthy of further investigation, of research.

Six of the eight chapters have previously been published as follows: "Logical Structure of English Sentences," in *Language, Belief, and Metaphysics*, edited by Howard Kiefer and Milton Munitz (Albany: State University of New York Press, 1970), 25–36 (copyright © 1970 by the State University of New York, reprinted by permission of the State University of New York Press); "A Response to 'Stimulus Meaning,'" *The Philosophical Review*, LXXIX, 1 (January, 1970), 63–74; "On H. P. Grice's Account of Meaning," *Analysis*, XXVIII, 1 (October, 1967), 1–8; "Natural and Formal Languages," in *Language and Philosophy*, edited by Sidney Hook (New York: New York

University Press, 1969), 223–240 (© 1969 by New York University, reprinted by permission of New York University Press and the University of London Press Limited); "Understanding," in *Studies in Thought and Language,* edited by Joseph L. Cowan (Tucson: University of Arizona Press, 1970), 65–77 (copyright 1970, reprinted by permission); "What Is Said," in *Semantics of Natural Language,* edited by Gilbert Harman and Donald Davidson (Dordrecht, Holland: D. Reidel Publishing Company, 1972), 709–721 (reprinted by permission).

Douglas Stalker has been of much help to me in my research. I am also indebted to him for preparing the index. And I am greatly indebted to Claire Miller for her constant secretarial care.

PAUL ZIFF

Chapel Hill

Contents

Understanding
Understanding

Così è (se vi pare)

I

Understanding

On occasion some of us are concerned to understand what is said. What is it that we are then concerned to do? To understand, of course, but what is that?

This question, so cast, can invite the blankest of stares, but it can be construed: let something be said to two persons such that, though each heard it, one did but the other did not understand what was said. Presumably there was some difference then and there between these two that obtained simply because one did and the other did not understand what was said. What was that difference?

The difference between one who understood and one who did not need not have been a difference in actual overt behavior, verbal or nonverbal.

If each heard what was said even if neither gave any indication, neither responded in any way, possibly one did and the other did not understand. If this were so perhaps we would not know that one did and one did not understand. But that possibility would remain: such is our common conception of understanding.

Perhaps the difference is that though neither did anything in any way noticeable or overt or evident, one could have done something of that sort that the other could not, thus a difference in potential overt behavior. For suppose what had been said was 'Open the safe: the combination is left 23, 4, 21.' Then perhaps the one who understood could have opened the safe and perhaps the other could not.

But as against this it is conceivable that, with respect to such overt behavior as opening a safe, the one who did not understand what was said could nonetheless have done what the other could have done, and it is conceivable that the one who did understand could not have done anything that the other could not have done. For first, the one who did not understand might already have known the combination to the safe and so could have opened the safe even though he had not understood what was said; second, each could have been encased in concrete with only ears protruding and these rendered immobile and so since neither could have done anything noticeable or overt or evident, the one who understood could not have done anything of that sort that the other could not.

To claim that the difference between one who understood what was said and one who did not was not a difference in overt behavior, either actual or potential, verbal or nonverbal, is not to deny that there was, in the case in question, something which the one who did not understand could not possibly have done which possibly the one who did understand could have done. For only the one who understood could possibly have obeyed the given order.

If the one who understood the order to open the safe were then to have opened the safe, in so doing he would have been obeying the order. Whereas if the one who had

not understood what was said had nonetheless then opened
the safe, in so doing he would not have been obeying the
order even though it could certainly have seemed as though
he were.

But such a difference makes no difference here. The
difference between obeying an order to open a safe and
merely behaving in a way that constitutes compliance with
an order to open a safe is not an overt behavioral difference.

Understanding what is said is, in the respects noted,
somewhat on a par with having a pain. For just so there is
no piece of overt behavior, either actual or potential, that
inevitably serves to differentiate between a man who is in
pain and one who is not. There is nothing that a man
who is in pain does or can or could do that is noticeable or
overt or evident that a man who is not in pain could not
do equally well.

Understanding what is said is also like having a pain in
that just as some minor pains, say a slight pain in one's
head, can hardly be specifically manifested in overt behavior, just so one who understands what is said when
what is said is something like 'The Löwenheim-Skolem
theorems have remarkable implications,' can hardly specifically manifest his understanding in overt behavior. Just as
there is no specific overt behavior that is indicative of a
slight pain in one's head, so there is no specific overt behavior that is indicative of an understanding of any of
innumerable statements.

But understanding is in a way worse than pain. For
though neither understanding nor pain need be evidenced
nor can be unmistakably evidenced by overt behavior, at
least a person in pain can hardly have much doubt whether

he is in pain: he has the pain, he experiences pain. But one who understands what is said need not experience anything at all and on occasion he may be in considerable doubt whether he understands what is said.

Since evidently there need not have been either an actual or potential overt behavioral difference between one who understood what was said and one who did not, if there was any difference between two such persons we must look elsewhere to find it. Is it that the one who understood what was said, say *S*, made an inference from *S*, whereas the one who did not understand did not?

How are we here to construe making an inference from *S*? If someone says 'It is raining' and I then say 'Then we shall have to call off the game,' my so saying could be held to exemplify the making of an inference. But my actually saying this is in itself merely another piece of overt behavior, verbal rather than nonverbal, but still not to the present point. Suppose, however, on hearing what is said I then think, it then in consequence occurs to me, that then we shall have to call off the game. This could be held to constitute the making of an inference. Let us say that to make an inference from *S*, where *S* is something that is actually said, is to infer *P* from *S*, where *P* is something expressible in words and having some of the properties of its verbal expression; in particular, it too may be understood just as its verbal expression may be understood, and if its verbal expression can be associated with a truth value, so it too can be. (In traditional terms I suppose *P* would thus correspond more or less to an "entertained proposition" at the moment of festivity.)

Is it that one who understood *S* must have made an inference from S? There is, I think, no reason to think it. Let S be a query about the time; if I understand S, I may simply glance at a watch and then say what time it is by way of reply. In introspection one is not apt to find any indication that any inference was made. (Possibly here some could be inclined to speak of an "unconscious inference" but little is likely to be gained by doing so.)

Is it that the one who understood S was able to make an inference from S whereas the one who did not was not? This can hardly be correct but, as will be seen, the question is somewhat complex.

To begin with, one can have good reason to believe that S is a statement having a truth value even if one does not understand S. Thus one may have good reason to believe that a person who said 'Differential puffing is an expression of differential *in situ* transcription' in so saying made a statement having a truth value even if one does not understand the statement one believes to have been made.

The question whether one is able to make inferences from a statement if and only if one understands it is complicated by the fact that understanding admits of degrees. One may fully understand or one may only partially understand, or understand roughly, or only more or less. To hope to have some understanding of a statement is not to be overambitious.

A man who has no conception of what differential puffing is may hear and not understand the statement in question. But to claim that he does not understand that statement is not to deny that even so he may have some understanding of what was said. He may have some understanding of it but not enough to warrant the unqualified claim that he does understand it, and his understanding of it may be sufficiently insufficient to warrant the unqualified claim that he does not understand it.

That one may be able to make an inference from what is said even if one does not understand it may be argued in three different ways on the basis of three different kinds of examples. Let what is said be 'Differential puffing is an expression of differential *in situ* transcription' and let this be S.

First, one who does not understand S may nonetheless be able to infer P from S, where P is expressible as 'Something is an expression of something.' For though his understanding of S is sufficiently insufficient to warrant the unqualified claim that he does not understand S, he may know that if S is true then P must be true.

But in reply it may be said that the case supports rather than confounds the claim that one is able to make an inference from S only if one understands S. For though it is true that the man in question can rightly be said not to understand S, he nonetheless has some understanding of S, and it is that aspect of S that he does understand that accounts for the inference he is able to make. Thus the inference he is able to make is as it were in some sense proportional to his understanding of S.

Second, one who does not understand S may know that S is a statement having a truth value and so he may be able to infer P from S, where P is expressible as 'Some statement, that could be made by uttering the words "Differential puffing is an expression of differential *in situ* transcription" in some appropriate way and under appropriate conditions, would be true.'

But in reply it may be said that the inference to P is not an inference from S but rather an inference from the fact that a certain speech act was performed by uttering certain words. It is not what was said that warrants the inference to P but simply the fact that something was stated by using certain words.

Third, one who does not understand S may know that S is a statement having a truth value and so he may be able to infer P, where P is expressible as 'Either differential puffing is an expression of differential *in situ* transcription or snow is white,' and this on the grounds that from any S having a truth value one may infer the disjunction S *or* Q.

Against this it may be argued that one has not made a genuine inference from S if, as we are supposing, one does not understand S; for if one does not understand S one does not understand the disjunction S *or* Q either: if one is genuinely to infer P that which is inferred must itself be understood.

If the replies just indicated were correct, it would follow, I think, that one is not able to make an inference from a statement that one does not understand. And this is to say that being able to make an inference from S would be a sufficient condition for understanding S. But if this were so the reply just given to the third argument must be inadequate to the point at issue.

One who knows some elementary logic and knows merely that S is a statement having a truth value is able to infer P from S, where P is expressible as a statement of the form:

S or Q_1 or Q_2 . . . or Q_n, where the *Q*'s are such statements as 'Snow is white,' 'The sky is blue,' and so forth. (Although one may plausibly argue that one does not understand the disjunction *S or Q* if one does not understand one of the disjuncts, one cannot plausibly argue that one does not understand the disjunction *S or* Q_1 *or* Q_2 . . . *or* Q_n simply in virtue of the fact that one does not understand one disjunct. If one understands all but a single sentence of a lengthy novel, should one say that one did not understand the novel?) That the one who infers *P* from *S* understands *P* is then indicated by the fact that he is able to make inferences from *P*. And since he is able to infer *P* from *S*, he must understand *S*, contrary to our original hypothesis. This would mean that knowing some elementary logic and knowing merely that *S* is a statement having a truth value is sufficient for understanding *S*. Since this is clearly absurd, it is equally clear that being able to make an inference from *S* is not a sufficient condition for understanding *S*.

Is being able to make an inference from *S* a necessary condition for understanding *S*? That is, if one understands *S* does it follow that one is able to make an inference from *S*?

Let it be clear what the letter '*S*' is here supposed to designate. The letter '*S*' is here being used for the moment in connection with the present example to designate a statement that we are supposing to be made at a certain time and place. Thus '*S*' here refers to a statement associated with a supposed temporal event, with the performance of a particular declarative speech act. Suppose another statement is made at a different time or place such that this statement is sufficiently similar in the relevant respects, whatever they may be, to warrant classing this statement as a statement of the same type as the first. Let 'S_i' designate the statement made. In so far as we are here concerned with questions of understanding, we cannot here identify S_i with S. The reason for this is simply that even though one might understand S, it does not follow that one understands S_i: it is fortunately the case that, even if one does not understand a statement at one time, one may manage to understand its equivalent at a later time. To take account of such a possibility, we are here using the letter 'S' to designate a statement at a particular time and place such that no recurrence of S itself is possible. Thus we are concerned with what may be called "statement-tokens" rather than "statement-types".

On the hypothesis in question, if a man understands S he is able to infer P_i from S, where P_i is expressible by some statement-token or other, possibly one of the same type as S. For this to be a genuine inference, however, he would have to understand P_i. To understand P_i on the hypothesis (and on our assumptions about making an inference), he would also have to be able to infer P_j from P_i. And so of course he would have to be able to infer P_k from P_j, and so on *ad infinitum*. This means that to understand S, he would have to be able to make not just one but all of an infinite series of inferences.

It is essential to realize that what is required here is not simply that the man be able to make any inference of the infinite series but that he be able to make all of the inferences, for if he cannot make all, he cannot make any. For suppose a man is able to make any but not all of the inferences of the series from S to P_1 to P_2 to . . . . Since he is not able to make all of the inferences, there must be an inference, I_i, that he is not able to make. This means that there must be a P_i in the series such that he is not able to make the inference from it. (It won't do to argue here that since by hypothesis he is able to make any inference of the series, he must be able to make them all, and this on the grounds that since he can make any inference, P_i cannot be P_1 since he is able to infer P_2 from P_1, and P_i cannot be P_{n+1} since he can infer P_{n+1} from P_n. If an usher has only 10 seats available and 11 people to be seated, though he is able to seat any one of the group, he is not able to seat them all. If he is not able to seat them all then there is at least one member of the group that he is not able to seat. Hence being able to seat any one of a group is not incompatible with not being able to seat some one of the group.) That the man in question is not able to make the inference from P_i means that on the hypothesis in question he does not understand P_i, and hence the inference to P_i was not itself a genuine inference. From which it follows that he was not able to make inference I_{i-1} either. From which it follows that he was not able to make the inference from P_{i-1}, and thus not able to make the inference from P_{i-n}. and so not able to make any inference from S. Thus if he cannot make all of the inferences of the series, he cannot make any. (The analogous difficulty could be created for an usher who has only 10 seats but 11 people to be seated if he were instructed that he is not to seat a person unless he is also able to seat an unseated friend of the person. Suppose all 11 people waiting to be seated are friends, and suppose 10 of them are then hastily seated by the usher. There was, as there was bound to be, one person, P_i, who was not seated. But if so, P_i's friend P_{i-1} was seated in violation of the rule that he was not to be seated unless his unseated friend were also seated; on realizing this a conscientious usher would have to unseat P_{i-1}; but then of course he would have to unseat P_{i-2}, and so on. The consequence would be that the usher would not be able to seat anyone.)

Although it may seem strange to say so, it takes time actually to make an inference. It does not take much time. But the speed of conductivity in the brain indicates that 20 inferences per second is likely to be the upper limit that a human being is capable of. And a life expectancy of 65 years means that the upper limit for the number of inferences an average human being is able to make is in the neighborhood of forty-one billion (enough, no doubt, to pass the time).

Since there is a finite upper limit to the number of inferences a human being is able to make, and since the condition in question would require one to be able to make an infinite number of inferences, one must reject that condition. And this is to say that if being able to make an inference from a statement to a statement one understands were a necessary condition for understanding any statement, no one would understand any statement.

One could of course avoid this conclusion by not requiring that one understand that which is inferred and thus no further inference need be possible from that which is inferred. So construed, the condition that one be able to make such an inference from S if one understands S could perhaps more plausibly be supposed to be necessary, but it would be unilluminating since with a minimal understanding of logic one could always, for any statement whatever, infer the denial of its denial, and so forth.

The difference we are looking for is not to be found in the ability to make inferences; possibly it is to be found in the possibility of providing paraphrases. Is it that one who understands what is said could paraphrase what is said but one who does not could not?

That the ability to provide a paraphrase cannot suffice here as a sufficient condition for understanding what is said can be seen in a glance. If one has a thorough grasp of the syntax of a language then even if one has virtually no knowledge of its semantics one can nonetheless readily provide paraphrases. Thus without understanding S one can, on the basis of syntactic considerations alone, paraphrase it as 'Differential *in situ* transcription is something that differential puffing is an expression of' or as 'Differential *in situ* transcription and differential puffing stand in a relation such that the latter is an expression of the former.'

The view that being able to provide a paraphrase is a necessary condition for understanding what is said is a mare's nest.

Assuming that it is not altogether unclear what is to count as a paraphrase, to provide a paraphrase of a statement, S, requires one to say (or to write) something, P, such that P is a paraphrase of S. If the condition in question were a necessary condition for understanding what is said it would follow that no nonhuman animal we know of ever understands anything that is said. (Don't horses and dogs on occasion understand and obey spoken commands? That either makes inferences is doubtful; that neither could provide paraphrases is certain.) Furthermore, it would follow that such creatures as infants and unlettered mutes cannot understand anything that is said.

To suppose that being able to provide a paraphrase is a necessary condition for understanding what is said is to suppose that one cannot understand a use of words unless one is oneself able to use words. But there is no reason to think that and good reason not to.

The marshaling of evidence in support of the counter claim that one can understand a use of words even if one cannot oneself use words here admits of an avid eclecticism. Information theory, psychology, common sense, all lend credence to the view.

The phenomenon of being able to understand a foreign language but not to speak it, of being able to read it but not to write it, is not unusual. (An inability to speak in Italian need not be confused with an incapacity to speak. Leopardi *sensa lingua* would not be *sensa linguaggio*. But an unschooled tongueless Texan would lack both the capacity to speak and the ability to speak in Italian.)

Studies of aphasics indicate that two relatively distinct types can be discerned and that instances of each are in fact to be encountered: expressive aphasics and receptive aphasics. Expressive aphasics can understand a use of words but cannot themselves use words. Receptive aphasics cannot understand a use of words directed by others to them but can themselves use words.

The robot-minded among us are wont to construe using words and understanding a use of words in terms of encoding and decoding processes. It is not an impossible point of view.

If, in Martian manner, we think of the process of using words as an encoding process in which something, *a*, is encoded as something, *b*, it is not implausible to think of understanding a use of words as something connected with the completion of a decoding process. If so, the separation of the hearer from the speaker can seem immediate and complete. That one can decode *b* as *a* in no way necessitates one's having the ability to encode *a* as *b*. From an engineering standpoint, decoding and encoding are far from symmetrical processes: think of the differences between a television receiving station and a television broadcasting station. Receivers are not generally transmitters.

More precisely, think of a general all-purpose computer capable of computing the values of some function *E* (for encoding) and capable of computing the values of some function *D* (for decoding). Despite its capacity to compute both *E* and *D*, the machine may be programmed to compute *D* and yet not programmed to compute E. If the machine is programmed to compute *D* but not *E*, it is the analogue of a person who can understand but cannot speak a foreign tongue because of the lack not of a tongue but of the requisite knowledge, or better, "know-how". The analogue of the tongueless hearer can be supplied either by a suitably programmed but partially damaged all-purpose computer or by, what comes to much the same, a special-purpose computer having a relatively rigid structure rendering it incapable of computing the requisite function.

Our question is this: if two persons each heard and made out what was said but one did and the other did not understand it, what was the difference then and there between the two that obtained simply because one did and the other did not understand what was said? So far we have concluded that that difference was not a difference in overt behavior, actual or potential; neither was it a difference in an ability to make inferences; neither was it a difference in an ability to provide paraphrases. That it is not any of these things was, I think, plain to begin with even though

I have been at some pains to make it so. This travail could have been considerably curtailed had we come by another way, had we reflected on an ambiguity of the phrase 'to understand what is said'.

The ambiguity of the phrase arises from and is owing to the ambiguity of the subphrase 'what is said': for, among other things, 'what is said' may refer either to the utterance uttered or to the statement made. If while pointing to me a person says 'That person is in pain' what he has said in the sense of the utterance uttered is 'That person is in pain'; but what he has said in the sense of the statement made is that I am in pain.

We are here concerned with understanding what is said in the sense of understanding the statement made. We are not primarily concerned with understanding what is said in the sense of understanding the utterance uttered. But the difference between understanding the statement made and understanding the utterance uttered is not a difference with respect to understanding. The ambiguity of the phrase 'to understand what is said' does not arise from and is not owing to any ambiguity of the word 'understand'. The sense of that word here appears to be univocal. But if so, understanding what is said in either sense of the phrase can hardly sensibly be supposed to be a matter of behavior or of making inferences or providing paraphrases.

To understand what is said, in the sense of understanding the utterance uttered, is (not so simply) to hear and make out the utterance. Thus if from the lecture platform one asks students at the rear of the room 'Can you understand what is said?', the answer is yes if they can hear and make out the words: thus even Heidegger can hope to be understood. It is necessary merely not to mumble overmuch.

Understanding the utterance uttered would then appear

to be a matter of data processing of some sort. A hearer is supplied with auditory data which are to be processed in such a way that, on completion of the processing, the hearer will have made a correct phonemic morphologico-syntactic identification and classification of the constituents of the utterance.

If a hearer does understand the utterance uttered in the ordinary run of things one would expect him to be able somehow to utilize this knowledge. And in the ordinary run of things hearers on occasion do utilize such knowledge in supplying verbatim reports. But an exercise of the ability to supply a verbatim report depends on factors over and above a knowledge of what was said. And on occasion, as in the case of aphasics, or of mutes, and so forth, hearers may lack the requisite abilities even though they have the requisite knowledge. That the means of expression are not available to a hearer cannot ever suffice to establish that he lacks the requisite knowledge to be expressed.

Understanding what is said, in the sense of understanding the statement made, also appears to be essentially a matter of data processing of some sort. Again a hearer is supplied with auditory data which are to be processed in such a way that, on completion of the processing, the hearer will have made a correct semantic identification and classification of the constituents of the statement made.

If the hearer does understand the statement made then in the ordinary run of things one would expect him to be able somehow to utilize this knowledge, either in the modulation of overt behavior, or in making inferences, or in providing paraphrases. And in the ordinary run of things hearers on occasion do so perform. But again an exercise of the abilities requisite for so performing depends on factors over and above a knowledge of the statement made. And again on occasion a hearer may lack either the opportunity or the requisite capacities or abilities even though he has the requisite knowledge.

That understanding what is said is essentially a matter of data processing of some sort is not a claim about the use of words. What is at issue here is our conception of understanding, not our use of the word 'understand'. But support for the view being urged can be gained by considering why we use that word as we do.

Suppose there is at hand a concrete slab with an inscription carved on it. The inscription reads: "Take two paces forward, three to the left, four more forward, six to the right, and then salaam!" A man who had paused to look at the slab then did precisely that, swiftly and surely. How are we to account for the fact that he behaved in precisely that peculiar fashion? To suppose he just happened to behave so would be to suppose a minor miracle had taken place.

Since his peculiar behavior occurred immediately subsequent to his having attended to the inscription, and assuming that no equally attractive alternative explanation is available, to explain what would otherwise appear to be a miraculous coincidence between the immediate significance of the inscription and the evident modulation of his behavior, we must suppose that the visual data he was supplied with were somehow rendered efficacious by means of some internal processing. We baptize such successful processing 'understanding' and we attribute to him an understanding of what was inscribed.

To realize that understanding what is said is essentially a matter of data processing of some sort is not, unfortunately, enough to achieve a clear conception of what understanding is. For one wants to know precisely what the character and form of that processing is.

Unhappily the character and form of the data processing that can culminate in understanding is today much of a mystery. But one important feature of our present conception of understanding can readily be discerned.

To understand what is said, in the sense of understanding the utterance uttered, is to hear and make out the words. Thus in effect one performs a morphological analysis of the utterance; the utterance is segmented, decomposed into its morphological constituents. The data processing that can culminate in understanding has a specific character: it is an analytic process. Understanding, not surprisingly, is akin to figuring out, deciphering, decoding, and the like.

Further support for the view that the process is essentially analytic in character can be uncovered with the following sort of question. Suppose we have before us the concrete slab on which there is a carved inscription. Then although we can perhaps set ourselves the task of attempting to understand the carved inscription, we cannot set ourselves the task of attempting to understand the slab: a concrete slab cannot be understood and not of course because it is inscrutable. But why can't the slab as well as the carved inscription be understood?

I have claimed that understanding is essentially a matter of analytical data processing of some sort. This in turn may suggest that the reason why the inscription can but the slab cannot be understood is that the inscription can but the slab cannot be processed in the appropriate way, whatever that way may prove to be. But that won't do at all.

First, it is not the carved inscription but the visual data supplied by the inscription that can be processed. Second, a slab certainly can supply visual data that can be processed in an appropriate way, whatever that way may be; for one may attempt to understand and one may succed in understanding the structure of the slab on the basis of a visual inspection.

A concrete slab may have a complex structure: it may be reinforced, pretensed, and so forth. And this structure can perhaps be understood. And yet the reason that one cannot, without linguistic deviation, speak of "understanding a slab" is that only that which is composite, complex, and thus capable of analysis, is capable of being understood. Even though a slab may in fact be something composite, complex, to speak of it as "a slab" is to speak of it as something uncomplex, unitary. Suppose, on encountering a concrete slab lying in a field, one were told to count it. Assume that one was not then in the process of counting concrete slabs lying about. Possibly one might respond to the order by saying "One!" but even that seems somewhat absurd. And yet a slab is a collection of molecules and one might madly enough be enjoined to count the molecules of the collection.

If one is to speak sensibly of "understanding" something, that which is to be understood must be characterized in such a way as to indicate that it is capable of the requisite sort of analytical data processing. So one speaks of understanding a statement, an utterance, a person's behavior, the structure of a slab and so forth. (We do speak of "understanding a person" but this is a matter of understanding his behavior, personality structure and so forth; the expression is an evident trope on a par with "believing a person" which is a matter of believing what he says.)

To understand that understanding is the resultant of some sort of analytical data processing is to have some understanding of understanding. But not much and not enough to warrant an unqualified claim to understand understanding.

More could be conjectured here, albeit somewhat airily. Unquestionably the process in question involves synthesis as well as analysis: the utterance that is understood is analyzed into words but synthesized into a sentence. But to understand the nature of this synthesis we shall have to have a much clearer conception than we have at present of the constitution and character of the set of elements to be synthesized. In understanding what is said, in the sense of understanding the statement made, we shall have to have a clearer conception of the elements of the analysis, of the set of factors that serve to determine the immediate significance of the utterance uttered. Furthermore, if we are to understand the processes involved in understanding what is said, we shall have to disentangle them from the little-known and ill-understood processes involved in perception. There too, one supposes, the data are subject to some sort of systematic synthesis. Consideration of perceptual processes is of course inescapable in so far as understanding what is said requires one to hear (or at least to witness something in connection with) what is said.

When one broaches such topics as these, one can no longer avoid the dismal conclusion that to understand understanding is a task to be attempted and not to be achieved today, or even tomorrow.

II

What Is Said

Some of us sometimes understand some of what is said. The problem is to understand how we manage to do this. The matter is complex. No reasonably complete answer is at present possible. We maunder about in ignorance. But only the barest speculative sketch is aimed at here: a few possible bones will be provided on which flesh may someday be hung.

We are concerned with what is said, to understand how it is we manage to understand it. But to speak of what is said is to babble with three tongues. These must be untangled.

To say something, in the ordinary course of things, one utters an utterance having a phonetic, phonemic, morphological, syntactic and semantic structure and one utters it under certain conditions. (No doubt one can also be said to say something by means of gestures alone, or by a shake of the head, or by signaling, telegraphing and so forth, but such matters need not detain us here.) The minimum requirement for having said something appears to be that the utterance be constituted of, or significantly correlated with, words in some language or other: utterances that fault this condition are mere mouthings, moans or shrieks; the utterer is not a speaker. Whereas if someone utters an utterance of the form 'Dog the table banana is,' something was said, albeit something nonsensical: that the utterance is a morphological morass does not matter, that it have a morphological structure does.

In thick guttural accents one utters the utterance 'I vant a banana': what has he said? He has said this: 'I vant a banana.' In reporting what is said in this sense one apes the speaker, emulates a tape recorder.

One who utters the utterance 'I vant a banana' can also be said to have said 'I want a banana.' And such a report is commonly classed a "verbatim" report of what was said. Again, a verbatim report of what is said when a person utters the utterance 'I study *economics*' could well be 'He said "I study *economics*"': in verbatim reporting one generally discounts phonetic and phonemic differences. And, as one would expect, the discounting of phonemic differences can on occasion give rise to borderline cases: if the Reverend Spooner were to have uttered the utterance 'I spike liders,' one could say that what he said in the verbatim sense was 'I like spiders.' But if he had uttered the utterance 'I saw a flutterby butterfly,' would one say that he had in the verbatim sense said 'I saw a butterfly flutterby'? Or would one say that what he had said in the verbatim sense was 'I saw a flutterby butterfly' but that is not what he meant to say?

What is said is slippery stuff: one readily slides not only over phonetic and phonemic differences but over morphological differences as well. A person who says (in the verbatim sense) 'I want a banana' can also be said to have said that he wants a banana. Thus if George says 'I want a banana' and Josef says 'He wants a banana,' where the reference is to George, then each has said the same thing, namely that George wants a banana. Or if George says 'Maybe there are no bananas' and Josef says 'Perhaps there ain't no bananas' then again each has said the same thing, despite the morphological differences between the utterances uttered.

Syntax is here no more sacrosanct than morphology. If in response to the query 'Who ate the cake?' one man says 'The man,' another 'The man did it,' another 'The man ate the cake,' another 'The cake was eaten by the man,' then each has said the same thing.

Semantic features are also subject to slough. In particular to begin with, reference may go by the board. If George says 'I am tired' and Josef says 'I am tired' then each has said the same thing, namely, that he is tired. To count George and Josef as having here said the same thing is to discount the evident referential differences between the sentences uttered. There are even more extreme cases: suppose one person says 'The house is green,' another says 'My jacket is green,' another 'The car is green,' and so on; in a sense they are all saying the same thing, namely, that certain things are green.

Just as referential differences may be discounted, so one may discount differences between the specific characterizations supplied. Suppose different persons offer the following reports about a UFO: 'The object had at least thirteen faces,' 'The object had sixteen faces,' 'The object had many sides,' 'The object had more than thirteen but less than twenty faces'; in a sense they are all saying the same thing, namely, that the object was a polyhedron. The sense of 'what is said' is further attenuated when one simultaneously discounts both referential differences and differences between the specific characterizations supplied. If one person says 'My car is green,' another 'The house is blue,' another 'His jacket is yellow,' and so on, in a sense they are all saying the same thing, namely, that certain things are colored.

An automatic consequence of discounting referential differences is that differences in truth are simultaneously discounted. For if George says 'I am tired' and Josef says 'I am tired' then, in the sense in which what is said is one and the same, one cannot say that what is said is either true or not true. For what each said was that he was tired. And is that true? For what if George was in fact tired and Josef was not? Then what was said was neither true nor not true, but what was said was true of George, not true of Josef.

But one may also discount differences in truth without discounting referential differences. On Monday I say 'My house is red' and my house is red. Then on the following Wednesday I say 'My house is red' but my house is no longer red because the house was painted on Tuesday. Then discounting questions of truth, what I said on Monday is the same as what I said on Wednesday. It may seem, however, as though this case were not to the point: one may be inclined to say that, despite my disclaimer, what was said on Monday and what was said on Wednesday can be counted as one and the same only by discounting referential differences. For there was, so it may seem, a covert reference not to my house but to my house on a specific day. Thus on Monday I said that my house on Monday was red whereas on Wednesday I said that my house on Wednesday was red. One can take such a line. But why should one? One can just as well, or better, say that what was said was one and the same and that the reference was in each case the same, to the house simply and not to the house on Monday or Wednesday. And then what was said was neither true nor not true though what was said was true of the house on Monday, not true of the house on Wednesday.

Finally, the expression 'what is said' has such a use that one can in fact transcend every linguistic feature of the utterance uttered. If on being asked to play tennis George replies 'I have work to do' and Josef replies 'Do I look like an athlete?' then perhaps each has said the same thing, namely, no. This sense of 'what is said' may be baptized the "implication" sense.

There are, it appears, a great many factors serving to determine what is said. But apart from the mimicking, verbatim and implication senses, it appears that certain syntactic and semantic factors are essential with respect to the other senses of 'what is said.' If George says (in the verbatim sense) 'They are leaving' and Josef says 'They are going' then each has said the same thing, namely, that they are departing (or that they are leaving or that they are going). But if George says (in the verbatim sense) 'Why is he slipping?' and Josef says 'Why is he slipping?' then even though they have said the same thing in the verbatim sense, it seems that they have not said the same thing in any other sense (mimicking and implication senses aside) for they have not said anything (mimicking, verbatim and implication senses aside). If George and Josef each say 'Why is he slipping?' one could report of them 'They asked the same thing, namely, why he is slipping' but not of course 'They said the same thing, namely, why he is slipping.' One can speak of what is said, in other than the mimicking, verbatim and implication senses, only if in uttering the utterance the speaker made some sort of statement or assertion or the like; the utterance must be in declarative form. Consequently, I propose to lump all such senses together under the rubric of the "statement" senses of 'what is said.'

I have indicated that I am concerned to understand how it is that we understand what is said. But one can now hear my words falling short of their mark. For of course I am also concerned to understand how it is that we understand what is asked and what is commanded and the like. Unfortunately there is no nice phrase for the purpose. Ignoring such niceties, if we are to understand how it is that we understand what is said, the first step would be to gain some insight into the character and operation of the factors that serve to determine what is said.

Some of the factors that serve to determine what is said are obvious enough: phonetic, phonemic, morphological, syntactic, semantic and contextual factors are all evidently at play. But not everything that serves to determine what is said can be listed, enumerated. To understand what is said it need not be enough to know and understand the language in which what is said is said. And this is always so when what is said is said by implication, i.e., is said in the implication sense of 'what is said.'

What is said by implication can be anything at all, other than what is in fact then said in the statement sense. To understand what is said by implication it is not enough to understand what is said in the statement sense. One may have to have some knowledge of the speaker's beliefs, attitudes, convictions, opinions and so forth. If on being asked to play tennis a person replies 'I have work to do,' what has he said by implication? That depends on him: no general answer is possible here. If the speaker is an ordinary sort then perhaps he was saying by implication that he couldn't play. But he needn't be an ordinary sort. Perhaps he's a queer sort who plays and is delighted to play only when he has work to do. If I know this about him and he knows I know it, then by implication he has managed to say that he would be delighted to play. Or what if he had replied 'It is snowing in Tibet'? Then possibly again he has managed to say that he would be delighted to play, but that would depend on him and on my knowledge of his quirks and his knowledge of my knowledge and so forth. Any fact known to us may be a factor serving to determine what is said by implication, but such factors cannot be effectively enumerated.

One may suppose, however, that what is said, in any literal sense other than the implication sense, is some function of some reasonably definite finite set of factors. For example, what is said in the mimicking sense appears to be a relatively simple function of the acoustic shape of the temporally ordered sequence of morphs constituting the utterance. Indeed, a tape recorder may be taken as constituting a physical realization of the function in question.

Such an account however is at once seen to be seriously deficient when one attends to the fact that no reference has been made to the matter of morpheme identification: a tape recorder makes no discrimination between mere mouthings and utterances having sufficient morphological structure to count as sayings. Among the factors serving to determine what is said, even in the mimicking sense of 'what is said,' must be included those factors, whatever they may be, that serve to identify the morphemes in question. If someone utters an utterance of the form 'Whadjamean?' then in the verbatim sense he may have said 'What do you mean?'; but if someone utters an utterance of the form 'Tadjageam' then possibly he has not said anything at all either in the mimicking or the verbatim senses of 'what is said.' And presumably the relevant difference between the two utterances is this: there is a relatively smooth curve leading from 'Whadjamean?' to 'What do you mean?' but there does not appear to be any smooth curve leading from 'Tadjageam' to any sequence of English morphemes. (Though I suppose one could try to pair 'Tadjageam' with 'Tied your game!': it is not irrelevant that it is difficult to find a short sequence of English phones that cannot conceivably be mapped on to some sequence of English morphemes.) In consequence one takes 'Whadjamean?' to be a sequence of English morphs, but 'Tadjageam' to be simply a sequence not of English morphs but at best of English phones.

But all talk of "smooth curves" is of course here at best figurative; at the worst, it is whistling in the dark (otherwise known as metaphysics). Among the factors that serve to determine what is said are those that serve to identify the morphemic constitution of an utterance. But such factors are not at present to be detailed: one glimpses them through a glass darkly.

If one peers into the workings of discourse, one can discern some sort of coherence factor at work serving to identify the morphemic constitutions of utterances. Consider the sentence 'He refused to have anything to do with the girl.' 'Refused' is an homonymous expression: there is one word having to do with declining and another having to do with installing another fuse. Even so, apart from special discourses, one can hardly construe the preceding sentence as having the same meaning as the sentence 'He

installed another fuse to have anything to do with the girl'
for the latter sentence, unlike the former, is syntactically
deviant. The reason for that is, of course, to be found in
the negative character of the homonym 'refuse' meaning
decline. (Note that such environments as 'He . . . ed to
have anything to do with the girl' can serve to establish the
existence of a class of negative words.) Now consider the
sentence 'He refused to marry the girl.' Here, unlike the
preceding case, immediate syntactic considerations do not
serve to impede a pairing of that sentence with a sentence
like 'He installed another fuse to marry the girl.' And now
consider the more complex sentence (or if you like, the
following pair of sentences) 'He refused to marry the girl;
he refused to have anything to do with her.' Although the
alternative of installing a fuse might at first seem to be
available in connection with the first occurrence of 'refused,'
it is more clearly not available in connection with the
second occurrence. In consequence, in the interest of
something like coherence, the alternative involving the in-
stallation of a fuse is somehow not available or not
genuinely available even for the first occurrence of 'refused.'

That there is some sort of coherence factor serving to
structure discourse should, I think, be fairly obvious. It is
indicated by all sorts of cases. For example, something like
coherence forces us to backtrack when we hear a sentence
like 'I watched her duck when they were throwing rotten
eggs; it swam out to the middle of the lake.' [1] Though one
may have begun by counting 'duck' as a verb, one will
probably end by counting it as a noun, and this in the
interest of coherence. The same sort of phenomenon is
exemplified by the (spoken) utterance 'He waxed Roth

[1] From Thomas Patton.

and then he waxed Smith.' [2] Still further evidence of a coherence factor is to be seen in the ease with which one can overcome ambiguities. For example, consider the following dialogue: 'When you said "refuse" did you mean install another fuse or did you mean decline? I meant decline. When you say "decline" do you mean sicken or do you mean lead down?' The second question is clearly absurd. The discourse is ostensibly concerned with homonyms of 'refuse'; although both 'install another fuse' and 'decline' are at once available as alternatives for 'refuse,' 'sicken' is not.

Apart from considerations of coherence, it is clear that such vague matters as general beliefs are relevant factors in morpheme identification. Consider the relatively unambiguous sentence 'My psychiatrist can lick your psychiatrist.' Despite the phonological fusion of morphologically distinct elements, all is likely to be relatively clear here: beat up, not treat like a lollypop, is what 'lick' looks to be. The identification of 'lick' as the lollypop morpheme is apparently hindered by the use of the word 'can.' Thus the sentence 'My psychiatrist licked your psychiatrist' can more plausibly be supposed to be ambiguous: either alternative is then perhaps available, though one is still more viable than the other. And certainly the sentence 'My cat licked your cat' is genuinely ambiguous. The explanation of all this is fairly obvious: since it is a common occurrence for one cat to lick in the lollypop sense another, or so it is generally believed, that sentence is at once ambiguous. And since it is generally easy to lick like a lollypop but not always so easy to beat, the use of 'can' serves to hinder one reading of 'lick' while facilitating the other.

[2] From Charles Hockett.

Apart from considerations of coherence and such vague matters as general beliefs, it is clear that nonlinguistic perceptual factors are also of considerable importance in morpheme identification. Given an appropriate perceptual situation, even if the actual morphs of the utterance are partially masked by noise or are markedly deviant in character, one need not encounter any difficulty in morpheme identification. The drunk waving his empty glass at you saying 'My grass's dry' is easily understood to have said in the verbatim sense 'My glass is dry'; but were an acoustically identical utterance to be uttered under different perceptual conditions, say while staring glumly at a drought stricken lawn, what would be said would, in the verbatim sense, be 'My grass is dry.'

One may suppose that what is said is some function of some reasonably definite finite set of factors but for the time being (and no doubt for some time to come) such a supposition is best seen as at best a heuristic maxim. Coherence, belief and perceptual factors perhaps are not computable and anyway do not at present admit of any plausible form of computation. But even if one could today discover a set of computable factors, the character of the requisite function would still pose a considerable problem.

In considering the sentence 'He refused to have anything to do with the girl' it was pointed out that one could hardly construe that sentence as having the same meaning as the sentence 'He installed another fuse to have anything to do with the girl' owing to the fact that the latter sentence, unlike the former, is syntactically deviant. Thus is appeared that syntactic factors sufficed to block the identification of 'refused' as the homonym meaning installed another fuse. More precisely, it might seem as though one could describe the situation as follows: first, syntactic factors served to delimit the choice for the environment 'He . . . ed to have anything to do with the girl' to negative morphemes; second, since only one of the homonyms having the shape 'refused' was a negative morpheme, namely that meaning decline, that one had to be and was then selected. But such an account of the situation would be excessively simple-minded.

The factors that serve to determine what is said have something of the character of vectors and what is said can be thought of as something of a vector sum. To suggest that the factors that serve to determine what is said can be thought of as vectors is, of course, at once to suggest that they can be represented by directed line segments, that they can sensibly be thought of as forces having a magnitude, a direction in some sort of linguistic space and a sense in which the direction is proceeding. It is also to suggest that one factor can, as it were, serve to deflect another. And more importantly, it is also to suggest that these factors may be active and operative even though owing to the interaction of other factors their action and operation may not be readily apparent.

Consider the sentences 'He barked his shin' and 'The dog barked.' These two 'bark's are homonyms: the former is a transitive verb, the latter intransitive. The former means skin, the latter yap. Consequently syntactic factors would seem to indicate that the meaning of 'He barked his shin' is much the same as that of 'He skinned his shin' and not the same as that of 'He yapped his shin.' Indeed this last sentence is clearly ungrammatical since 'yap' is an intransitive verb. To construe 'He barked his shin' as having much the same meaning as 'He yapped his shin' would, in consequence, be to construe the grammatical as the ungrammatical, the nondeviant as the deviant. So one may be inclined to suppose that 'He barked his shin' can't rightly be read as 'He yapped his shin.' But it can.

Syntactic structure constitutes a vector serving to determine what is said but this vector can be modified by the action of other vectors. In particular, there are discourse factors, vectors activated in discourse, that can serve radically to alter the reading of sentences. For suppose the sentence 'He barked his shin' were embedded in the following discourse: 'He was a remarkable ventriloquist. First, he made it seem that the cat was barking. Then he made the parrot bark. Then he barked a monkey, and then a shoe, then his hand, and then he barked his shin.' And do we understand what is being said? Of course we do. Nor is there much of a mystery about how we do it. Owing to the operation and action of a coherence factor we are impelled to read 'bark' as meaning yap. Then, in consequence, to allow for the intransitive role assigned to 'bark' in 'he barked a monkey' and 'he barked his shin', we are impelled to read 'barked a monkey' and 'barked his shin' as syntactic transforms of 'made a monkey bark' and 'made his shin bark,' thus allowing 'bark' to be fundamentally intransitive. Then owing to co-occurrence restrictions and to the operation of belief factors, we are impelled to read 'made his shin bark' as a transform of 'made it seem as if his shin barked.' In short, owing to the action of other vectors activated by the discourse in which the sentence is embedded, the sentence takes on an altered syntactic structure.

All factors serving to determine what is said appear to have a vectorial character. For example, the phonetic shapes of the elements of an utterance supply important factors serving to determine what is said. But the phonetic shapes of elements very often supply more than a single vector: the possibility of puns stems from the plurality of phonetic vectors supplied in a given utterance. Thus 'Armageddon awful fat' [3] is possible because of the phonetic vector supplied by the name which allows one to associate it with the phrase 'I am getting'; the reference of the name introduces a further vector which together with coherence and belief vectors serves to determine what is said, namely, that, as has been said, inside every fat man there is a thin man struggling to get out. Again, 'Madame was but a fly when Pinkerton spied her' [4] survives on vectors leading from 'but a fly' to 'butterfly' and from 'spied her' to 'spider' aided and abetted by belief factors connecting the lady with the lieutenant and the web he wove.

The same phenomenon can be witnessed at the morphemic level. Consider the sentence 'He squandered the rent': 'rent' is a homonym meaning roughly either a sum of money or a tear. If 'rent-1' is the word pertaining to money and 'rent-2 the word pertaining to a tear then one is inclined to say that 'rent-1' but not 'rent-2' occurs in the sentence 'He squandered the rent.' But how then shall we explain what is said if one says 'Her only dress was torn but he squandered the rent'? [5] For clearly 'rent-2' occurs in this sentence. I am inclined to suppose that a more plausible account of the situation is as follows: the phonemic sequence 'rent' supplies at least two vectors, one leading to the word 'rent-1' and the other to 'rent-2.' Generally one or the other vector is dominant, and only in the case of

[3] From Frank Sibley and Paul Ziff, *O Bitter Dicta* (Beirut: Punitive Press, 1960).
[4] *Ibid.*   [5] *Ibid.*

jokes or genuine ambiguities are both evident. Thus, on this view, even in a sentence like 'He always paid his rent on time' there is a vector leading to 'rent-2.' For again, one could reinforce that vector by embedding the sentence in some appropriate discourse, as in 'She allowed him to make rents in her dress, but only so long as he at once paid for the privilege: he always paid his rent on time.' Again, 'I want to buy some alligator shoes but I don't know what size my alligator wears' is a clear instance of a vector being reinforced by an appropriate discourse environment.

As I have elsewhere maintained, a word's having meaning in a language can be thought of in terms of the word's having associated with it a set of conditions, where a condition is taken to be that which is expressed by an open sentence, a predicative expression, or that which can be explicitly stated by employing a nominalized predicative expression.[6] Each of the associated conditions can be thought of as a vector invoked by each and every use of the word. But again, all such vectors can be opposed or reinforced by the action and operation of other vectors. As instances of metonymy, metaphor, synecdoche and so forth serve to indicate, any adequate account of the meaning of sentences and of their possible readings in a discourse must take into account the existence of what might be called certain standard discourse operators. Thus there is undoubtedly something like an irony operator that can be employed in a discourse to reverse, as it were, the sense of what is said. And so one can readily say 'bright' and have it mean stupid as in 'That was a bright thing to do: now we are completely without lights' said in reference to someone who has just blown all the fuses. To say 'bright'

[6] *Semantic Analysis* (Ithaca: Cornell University Press, 1960).

meaning hungry would be more of a feat. Note, however, that that can be done: there is what might be called a "nonce operator" available that serves to give a word a special meaning for the nonce. Thus one obtains what linguists call a nonce sense of a word.

The existence of discourse operators plays a fundamental role in the diachronic development of a lexicon. Owing to their continuing operation, the concept of a finite dictionary can at best be only something of a convenient myth: dictionaries are essentially open-ended (neither finite nor infinite), and the same is true of the sentences of a natural language like English: they are neither finite nor infinite; they do not constitute a definite set. Nonce uses apart, there is no reason to think of the meanings or of the senses of a word as constant: they are not. They may vary with the discourse. Languages flow in time; their slow drift can be seen in close in the easy deliquescence of conceptual limitations. If K is a bachelor it does not follow that K is incontinent; yet if one says 'That chary milkshop is surely not a bachelor!', one may be saying, among other things, that incontinence is a prerequisite for qualifying as a bachelor: the senses of words are easily so augmented. Or diminished: 'The pope is, you know, a bachelor, but perhaps not an eligible one.' Or fused into figures: 'The life of a married bachelor is, after all, not without its compensations.' ('A married bachelor' is an oxymoron, a figure of speech involving the union of contradictories; 'oxymoron' is derived from two Greek words, one meaning sharp or wise, the other meaning dull or foolish, thus 'oxymoron' is itself a type of oxymoron.)

Each of the conditions associated with a word constitutes a vector invoked by each and every use of the word.

But whether a particular vector is dominant depends on what other vectors are at play. Does it follow, for example, if K is a bachelor that K is not married? One can say that if George is a bachelor then if George is not a young knight, not a simple knight, not a yeoman of a trade guild, not a person who has taken a first degree at a university, and certainly not a young male fur seal, then if George is literally a bachelor, and if the word 'bachelor' is not being used in an augmented or diminished or in any way derivative or modified or shifted sense or meaning, then it does follow that George is not married. It does follow, which, despite the complications, is to say something of the form 'If a then it follows that b'; but then to say this is not, for example, to say that one is not apt to encounter sentences of the form or to the effect that a and not b, nor is it to say that such sentences if encountered, are not to be countenanced. We must eschew any too simple conception of how concepts are related and how words work together in sentences and discourses. If if a then it follows that b, then b is best thought of as a vector invoked by each and every utterance of a. The effectiveness of this vector in a particular context, whether its presence is to be felt and if it is, how and to what degree, depends on the other vectors also operative in the context. In consequence, claims of the form 'If a then it follows that b' cannot be easy either to refute or to confirm. For that b is often the case when a is also the case may be owing to the action not of a but of other vectors. Thus it is true that a tiger is a large carnivorous feline even though a new-born tiger is not a large carnivore and still is a tiger. And milk is an excellent food even though milk liberally laced with strychnine is milk but is not an excellent food.

The factors that serve to determine what is said, in every sense of that phrase, appear to constitute a hopelessly unmanageable motley. And even if one ignores what is said by implication, the factors serving to determine what is said (in the other senses of the phrase) still appear to be discouragingly disparate and complex. Linguistic, logical, psychological and perceptual factors are all evidently active and interactive. All such factors appear to function as vectors, but what the magnitudes or directions or senses of the different vectors are it is at present impossible to say. There is a cheerless moral to be drawn from all this: One may have a firm grasp of the phonology, morphology, syntax and semantics of a language, thus a thorough knowledge of the language, and yet not understand what is said in that language. But who would have thought otherwise?

III

The Logical Structure
of English Sentences

A sentence of English, of a natural language, has a logical structure but what its structure is is not always evident. And if it is not, it may be desirable to scan the sentence from a formal point of view, thus, in effect, to attempt a schematic representation of the English sentence as a sentence of a formal logic, the sentences of which bare their structure to the eye.

That a formal logic is of utility in connection with the logical analysis of a discourse is not to be doubted. A formal logic is an instrument for mapping a conceptual scheme, thus a device for subverting any plotted logical confusion. But any map must be read aright if it is to be of utility and any map may be misread and misreadings may give rise to misgivings about the value of the mapping enterprise. It is with such misreadings and misgivings that we shall be concerned here.

An uninterpreted formal system may be taken to be a finite collection of expressions of some appropriate sort together with various precise rules for their manipulation.[1]

[1] See, for example, Paul Cohen, *Set Theory and the Continuum Hypothesis* (New York: W. A. Benjamin, 1966) 3.

One can also think of such a system as constituted simply by various rules for the production of expressions of some appropriate sort together with precise rules for their manipulation. (Thus the formal system presented on pp. 56–68 of the volume of *The Journal of Symbolic Logic*, 5 [1940], in the library at Chicago Circle may then be said to be identical with the formal system presented on pp. 56–68 of the volume of *The Journal of Symbolic Logic*, 5 [1940], in the library at Princeton in that each is in accord with precisely the same rules.)

To provide an interpretation of a formal system is then to supply further rules that serve to establish relations between expressions of the formal system and various things or various matters. If a system admits of the principal interpretation required here, it is a logistic system. A formal logic is here construed as an interpreted formal logistic system. The principal interpretation required is that the well-formed formulas of the system be interpreted in such a way that their interpretations are, or are somehow associated with, what is true or what is false.

Different interpretations of the underlying formalisms can yield different logics. To illustrate: let '$p \supset p$' be a well-formed formula of an uninterpreted logistic calculus C. In providing an interpretation for C, we may let the letter 'p' be a variable for propositions that are either true or false; [2] or we may let 'p' be a variable for sentences that are either true or false,[3] in which case '$\supset$' may then be construed as a syntactic constant representing the result

[2] As in Alonzo Church, *Introduction to Mathematical Logic* (Princeton: Princeton University Press, 1956).

[3] As in Alfred Tarski, *Introduction to Logic* (New York: Oxford University Press, 1941).

of a specific operation over a pair of sentences to yield a single compound sentence; or we may let 'p' be a place holder for an arbitrary sentence, a dummy of a sort, in which case '⊃' need not be construed syntactically but may be interpreted as a sentence connective.[4] If C contains quantifiers, expressions of the form '(p)' or '(ηp)', then in case 'p' is construed simply as a dummy sentence, the quantifiers can be construed simply as asides to the effect either that it does not or that it does matter which sentence 'p' is a dummy for.

To provide a formal logical analysis of an English sentence, one may attempt to pair off the sentence with an expression of a formal logic. If the logistic system has been interpreted in terms of propositions, we shall have to suppose that the English sentence expresses a proposition and we shall have to find a proposition of the formal logic to pair off with it. If the system has been interpreted in terms of sentences, then we need not suppose that the sentence of English expresses a propostion, but we shall still have to find a sentence of the logic to pair off with it and we shall have to suppose that sentences may be either true or false.

Neither of these alternatives is particularly palatable. That declarative sentences of English express propositions is somewhat dubious; that such sentences are literally either true or false is even more dubious. The obvious difficulty is that declarative sentences of English are not invariant either with respect to the expression of propositions or

---

[4] As in Willard V. O. Quine, *Mathematical Logic* (New York: Norton, 1940), though Quine does not there actually present a formal uninterpreted calculus.

with respect to truth. If a sentence in one discourse is deemed to express a proposition, or to be true, another token of the same type (or if you prefer, another replica) in another discourse may express a radically different proposition, or may be false or even neither true nor false. For example, think of 'He is hungry' said in reference to George, who is hungry, in reference to Josef, who is not, and displayed (or voiced) here by way of an example. The proposition varies, the truth of what is said varies, but the logical structure of the sentence has presumably remained invariant.

This situation can, however, readily be remedied by supplementing our sentential interpretation of the formal system. Thus we further interpret the sentences of the logistic system as representatives of (or metonyms for) statements that are either true or false. I shall, however, in the interests of brevity, speak of sentences as true or false (and of predicates as true or not true of something), but this is to be understood as follows. To say that a sentence is true (or false), for example, to say that 'It is raining' is true (or false), is to say that the sentence token displayed (or voiced) here here represents a sentence token that may be uttered in some appropriate way under some appropriate conditions such that in uttering it the person uttering it is making a true (or a false) statement. It is to be further understood that though in fact the sentence token displayed (or voiced) here, the one about the weather, can equally well represent many different sentence tokens, some of which may be employed in making true statements and some in making false statements, if the sentence is here said to be true it is to be taken as representing only those tokens such that the utterance of the tokens does not exemplify an instance of semantic deviation and does constitute the making of a true statement. But rather than say all this every time, I shall simply speak of a sentence as being true or false.

To provide a logical analysis of a sentence of English one can attempt to pair off the English sentence with a sentence of a formal logic. The second member of such a pair can be thought of as a representation of the English sentence in the formal system. For example, to let 'p' stand in place of an arbitrary declarative sentence is not to assign much content to 'p', but such a representation is all that is required for the purposes of sentential logic. A consequence of this is that a representation of an English sentence in a sentential logic is essentially schematic in character; thus a representation of 'If it doesn't rain then it will snow' is '$\sim r \supset s$': this suffices to display a logical structure of the English sentence even though it conveys little of its content. Such a representation then constitutes a (partial) logical analysis of the English sentence.

In so far as there are different formal systems, each of which under an appropriate interpretation qualifies as a formal logic, it is evident that there can be no unique formal logical analysis of an English sentence. In consequence, such a sentence cannot have a unique formal logical structure. The best that one could hope is that a sentence have a unique formal logical structure relative to L, where L is some formal logic.

For example, let L_1 be a classical sentential logic and L_2 and intuitionistic sentential logic. For the sake of definiteness, let L_1 be the logic determined by axioms 1–7, 8°, and L_2 the logic determined by axioms 1–7, 8^I, in Kleene's *In-*

troduction to Metamathematics, sections 19, 23. Axiom 8°
is '$\sim\sim p \supset p$' and axiom 8^{I} is '$\sim p \supset (p \supset q)$'. Consider
the representation of 'If it doesn't rain then it will snow'
in L_1 and in L_2. Represented in L_1, the sentence takes the
form '$\sim r \supset s$'; represented in L_2, the sentence takes the
form '$\sim r \supset s$'. At a glance it may seem as though the structures thus assigned to the sentence were one and the same.
But that would be an illusion fostered by the notation.
The symbols '$\sim$' and '$\supset$' in L_1 cannot be identified with
the corresponding symbols in L_2. The symbols '$\sim$', '$\supset$',
'V', and '.' of L_1 are interdefinable; the corresponding symbols of L_2 are not. From '$\sim r \supset s$' in L_1 one can infer
'$\sim s \supset r$': no such inference is possible in L_2.

Another example: let L_1 and L_2 be equivalent sentential
logics differing only in that L_1 has a constant 'f' but '$\sim$'
does not appear as a primitive improper symbol, whereas
L_2 has no constant and '$\sim$' is a primitive. The representation of 'If it doesn't rain then it will snow' in L_1 takes the
form '$\sim r \supset s$', and in L_2 it takes the form '$\sim r \supset s$'. Here,
unlike the previous example, owing to the fact that L_1 and
L_2 are equivalent, there is no inferential difference between
the two representations. Nonetheless, the English sentence
has been assigned two different though equivalent structures, for in L_1, on the elimination of abbreviations,
'$\sim r \supset s$' takes on the form of '$(r \supset f) \supset s$'. (An analogue:
the structure of $a + (b + c)$ differs from that of $(a + b)$
$+ c$, but that difference makes no difference in ordinary
arithmetic.)

To represent an English sentence in a sentential logic is
not much of a problem though the inefficacy of such a representation in revealing the logical structure of the sentence
in question is, on occasion, not to be doubted. For example,

the discourse 'George ate: he ate and he ate and he ate and he ate' would seem to have the structure '$p . p . p . p . p$', which is equivalent to 'p'. But from the English discourse one can infer that George ate a great deal, not so from its logical representation. Again, from 'It snowed and it snowed and it snowed' one can infer that it snowed a great deal, not so from its logical representation. The reason for this lacuna in sentential logic is not hard to discern: the repetitive use of a verb in a discourse is equivalent to an adverbial modification of the verb. Sentential logic is not equipped to cope with adverbial modifiers. (Nor, for that matter, is quantificational logic, as we shall see.)

Matters become more complex, however, when one considers the representation of sentences in a first-order quantificational logic. Consider the sentence 'Something is gray'. In a standard first-order logic this sentence would take the form of '$(\exists x) [Fx]$'. Here it is necessary to consider what interpretation is being put on the formalism, thus what sort of logic one is working with.

We have assumed that the principal interpretation of a logistic system here is such that the well-formed formulas of the system are interpreted as sentences that are either true or false. If this is so, it must be allowed for by the interpretations assigned to the variables and constants of the system. This is usually accomplished by letting 'x' be a variable for individuals and letting the predicate (or predicative expression) 'Fx' denote what is called "the class that is the extension of the predicate". Under such an interpretation, sentences of the form '$(x) [Fx \supset Fx]$' prove to be logically true, and a sentence of the form '$(\exists x) [Fx]$' is true just in case there is something belonging to the class in question. But such an interpretation of the formalism poses philosophic problems, in particular, both so-called "ontological" problems and semantic problems.

First, to interpret '*Fx*' as denoting the class that is the extension of the predicate is to suggest or to seem to suggest that there are such things as classes that have an independent existence, that exist apart from a system of logic or apart from a language, thus to go along with what is currently known as a "Platonistic ontology". One who would be skeptical of such views should then be somewhat reluctant to employ such a logic. But second, to accept the representation as adequate is to accept the view, indeed a semantic theory, to the effect that the predicative expression 'is gray' denotes a class. I have strong feelings of no enthusiasm for such a theory. Fortunately there are viable alternatives.

One can alter the interpretation of the formalism. Thus we can let '*x*' be a variable for individuals while stipulating that '*Fx*' is to stand in place of an arbitrary predicative expression: we further stipulate that a sentence of the form '$(\exists x)$ [*Fx*]' is true just in case '*Fx*' is true of at least one individual. Thus rather than saying that '*Fx*' denotes something, we say it is true or false of something. (Here Quine has pointed the way in his many fine essays on these and related topics.)

A representation of 'Something is gray' will then take the form '$(\exists x)$ [*Gx*]', where '*Gx*' stands in place of the open sentence '*x* is gray'. A representation of 'Something is amiss' would then seem to take the form '$(\exists x)$ [*Ax*]'. On the intended interpretation, a sentence of that form is true just in case the predicate '*Ax*', that is, '*x* is amiss', is true of at least one individual. Since there is no individual that the predicate is true of, the sentence must be false, which is of course absurd, for here one could truly say that something is amiss. But to suppose that when one says that something is amiss one is saying that some individual is amiss is equally absurd. If we are to represent such English sentences in our formal logic, the logic will have to permit such a representation. This means that the interpretation of the formalism must be adapted to that purpose. In consequence, perhaps we cannot simply let 'x' be a variable for individuals. Or can we?

What we have touched upon here is not simply an anomalous sentence but a fertile field of discourse. Quine has said "The quantifier '$(\exists x)$' means 'there is an entity x such that', and the quantifier '(x)' means 'every entity x is such that' ".[5] This is of course to presuppose that 'x' has been interpreted as a variable for individuals, or entities or objects. A first order quantificational logic, so understood, would then seem to be a logic for those who would speak only of objects and object to any other way of speaking. Yet there are other sensible ways of speaking, which is not to say that there is an entity x such that x is a way of speaking.

To say 'There was an annular eclipse' is not to say that there was some individual or entity or object such that it was an annular eclipse. Eclipses are not entities but events. 'Eclipses exist' is a deviant sentence, which is not to deny that eclipses occur. 'There was a shot; whenever there is a shot, there is a reason to be wary: therefore there was a reason to be wary.' This would seem to be a reasonable piece of reasoning. But neither a shot nor a reason to be

[5] "On Universals," *The Journal of Symbolic Logic* XII (1947) 75.

wary can reasonably be characterized as an individual or an entity or an object, and a reason to be wary cannot reasonably be characterized as an event. And then there are such sentences as 'There is something wrong with the view', 'There is a time to speak and a time to be silent', and there is also no need to multiply examples beyond necessity.

I have said that a formal logic is an instrument for mapping a conceptual scheme. In constructing a map one inevitably adopts one form of projection or another, and one uses materials adequate to the purpose. On my map of the States, Arizona is red and the city of Phoenix is a deep red dot. But the state of Arizona is certainly not red, nor is it any other color, nor is Phoenix a dot. Better then to print a map of no color at all. But this would mean no map. Best learn to read the map.

What the ultimate constituents of the universe may be may be a matter for a cosmologist to ponder. But it need not exercise the talents of a logician concerned with the analysis of reasoning. We need not insist that '$(\exists x)$' is to mean 'there is an entity x such that': we could with equal grace and greater ease read it simply as 'there is an x such that'. But then what is 'x' a variable for? And this is like asking what color the map shall be, for it must be some color. So let 'x' be a variable for individuals or entities or objects, whatever you like. And so one will have to read the quantifier to mean 'there is an individual (or entity or object) x such that.' This need not occasion a resolute obmutescence: then to say 'there is an entity x such that Fx' is merely to adopt a logician's *façon de parler*.

The exigencies of a formal approach inevitably necessitate some blinking here and there. But it need not matter. A logician can close his eyes to the difference between an adjective and a noun phrase and no harm need be done. Thus a representation of 'Something is gray' and of 'Something is a map' will take the form of '($\exists x$) [Gx]' and of '($\exists x$) [Mx]', which means that both sentences have been assigned the same structure. (The difference in letters, 'M' in place of 'G', marks a difference in predicates, not a difference in structure.) But there does seem to be a difference in logical structure between these two English sentences, a difference that arises from and is owing to the fact that 'gray' is a predicate adjective whereas 'a map' is a noun phrase. And this difference appears to give rise to an inferential difference: to be a map is *ipso facto* to be an entity of some sort, but to be gray is not *ipso facto* to be an entity of some sort. The sentence 'Something is gray' is, I think, the sentence *par excellence* for logical parsing. But the undeniable difference between 'gray' and 'a map' makes no difference here. For if the predicate 'x is gray' is true of at least one individual then that which it is true of is bound to be an entity of some sort. Thus even though to be gray is not *ipso facto* to be an entity, anything that is gray is an entity (as much as anything that is "a so-and-so" is, as "a sky full of larks"). And so there is no reason to insist that the logic show a difference between 'Something is gray' and 'Something is a map'.

Blinking is one thing but blindness is another. Consider the sentence 'Something moves slowly'; one could represent this sentence as of the form '($\exists x$) [Sx]', where 'Sx' stands in place of 'x moves slowly'. Such an analysis would fail to assign structure to 'moves slowly'. In consequence, it would serve to block any attempt to account for the obvious truth of such a sentence as 'If a man moves slowly and another moves quickly then at least two men move'. One might attempt to cope with the matter by representing the sentence as of the form '$(\exists x)$ $[Sx.$ (z) $[Sz \supset Mz]]$', where 'Sx' stands in place of 'x moves slowly' and 'Mz' stands in place of 'z moves'. But this would mean that the sentence 'Something moves slowly' would be assigned the same structure as 'Something moves slowly and if anything moves slowly then it moves': that the logical structures of these two English sentences are identical is hardly credible. So long as 'Sx' stands in place of 'x moves slowly', the logical structure of the sentence appears to be simply that of '$(\exists x)$ $[Sx]$'; any supplementary clause would then serve to express an inference based on an analysis of the predicate 'Sx'.

It is fairly clear, I think, that the problem posed by the sentence 'Something moves slowly' is a general problem. It is occasioned by the fact that familiar quantificational logics are not equipped to cope with adverbs in any simple way. The basic form of sentences in a quantificational logic is '$(\exists x)$ $[Fx]$', and the simplest way to understand such an expression is to think of the letter 'F' as standing in place of a predicate adjective. The task of logical analysis, with respect to a familiar quantificational logic, is to make out that every expression is either the name of an individual or a predicate adjective at heart. And even the names of individuals need not appear in the final analysis. To put '$(\exists x)$' before 'Fx', thus to write '$(\exists x)$ $[Fx]$', is simply a way of indicating that 'Fx' does not always convert to a false closed sentence.

But adverbs in general are not adjectives at heart. (The contrary is more often the case. 'Utter' in 'He is an utter fool', 'fast' in 'He is a fast runner', 'perfect' in 'He is a perfect stranger', are adverbs in adjective's clothing.) Adverbs and adverbial objects operate on verbs, as does 'slowly' in 'He ran slowly'. Since the conspicuous operation in quantificational logic is that of predication, if one is to cope with the problems posed by adverbs, the only device available is to construe adverbial modification as an instance of predication. Thus one must cast 'slowly' in the guise of 'is slow', which means conjuring up an entity to fill the bill in 'x is slow'.

Since our logic requires us to conjure up entities, if we are to cope with adverbs, let us do so and see what they are like. Let us suppose that, among the things that can be values of our variables for individuals, we shall count such things as a run that was slow. One could then represent the sentence 'Something ran slowly' as '$(\exists x)\ (\exists y)\ [Pxy\,.\,Ry\,.\,Sy]$', where '$Pxy$' stands for '$x$ performed y', 'Ry' for 'y was a run', and 'Sy' for 'y was slow'. This is to construe running as a relation between a person and a run he performs. In this case such an analysis is readily seen to be essentially a *façon de parler*. We are not required to suppose that somehow runs have an existence of their own apart from things that run.

Yet I am inclined to think that such an analysis is on a par with an analysis of 'George is thinking of Josef' in terms of a relation between George and a thought, or an analysis of 'George thinks that Josef is dead' in terms of a relation between George and a propositional function in intension.[6] Both the phrases 'of Josef' and 'that Josef is

[6] Church's view; see his review in *The Journal of Symbolic Logic* V (1940) 163.

dead' are best seen as adverbial objects modifying the associated verbs. And of course the point in question is obvious in connection with one reading of the sentence 'George is hunting unicorns'. 'Unicorn' is then best seen as an adverbial object modifying the verb 'hunting'. In this case we can make that point clear by deleting the plural morpheme and placing the adverbial object before the verb and so saying 'George is unicorn hunting'. Analogously we might say 'George is of-Josef-thinking' and 'George that-Josef-is-dead-thinks'.

Another quite different move can be made to cope with adverbs. It too calls for conjuration. Following Reichenbach's lead, one can leap to a higher logic, introduce the letter 'f' as a variable for properties, and then solve the problem in a trice.[7] If something moves then it has one of the properties we may speak of as "motion properties". And to move slowly is then a matter of this property having the property of being slow. So we may represent 'Something moves slowly' as '$(\exists x) \ (\exists f) \ [fx \ . \ Mf \ . \ Sf]$'. Or as a variation on the theme, we can conjure up classes and class membership instead of invoking properties, in which case 'Something moves slowly' takes on the guise of '$(\exists x) \ (\exists \alpha) \ [x\epsilon\alpha \ . \ \alpha\epsilon M \ . \ \alpha\epsilon S]$'. The reference to properties or classes here is best seen as no more than a logician's device for sliding smoothly from 'slowly' to 'slow'. Yet it seems that such fictive entities are all too often supposed to have some independent reality.

Frege's famous analysis of 'x is an ancestor of y' takes the form of '$(\alpha) \ [y\epsilon\alpha \ . \ (z) \ (w) \ [w\epsilon\alpha \ . \ Fzw \ . \ \supset \ . \ z\epsilon\alpha] \ . \ \supset \ . \ x\epsilon\alpha]$'. Here there is explicit quantification over classes. (As

---

[7] See Hans Reichenbach, *Elements of Symbolic Logic* (New York: Macmillan, 1947) 301 ff.

it so happens in this particular case, it has proven possible to avoid such quantification by adopting Goodman's ingenious devices in his calculus of individuals. But as Goodman points out, the method does not work for the general case; in particular it does not yield an analysis of the ancestral of every two-place predicate of individuals.[8] But it is not difficult to see that the difficulties faced in an analysis of '*x* is an ancestor of *y*' are of a piece with those encountered in connection with adverbs in general. That George is an ancestor of Josef can, at least in part, be expressed by saying 'George is ancestrally related to Josef' (though this perhaps fails to make clear who is the ancestor of whom). To say that something moves slowly is to say how it moves. Just so, to say that George is ancestrally related to Josef is to say how he is related. And one could also say 'George is related to Josef, ancestorwise' (which could be a way of saying that they have a common ancestor): the colloquial affix '-wise' here serves to mark the noun 'ancestor' as an adverbial object.

Adverbs and adverbial objects are not the only source of special entities to be encountered in the course of logical analysis. Prepositional phrases make their own contribution: 'George came after Josef in ancestral succession', 'George came in a hurry and Josef left in a hurry, so both were in a hurry', and so forth. But the greatest share of all is undoubtedly contributed by nominalizations: a nominalization is at once the *bête noir* of a Nominalist and the pet of a Platonist.

The nominalizations of English that are particularly

[8] See Nelson Goodman, *The Structure of Appearance* (Cambridge: Harvard University Press, 1951) 40.

pertinent here are those dealing with predicate adjectives, for all such nominalizations can readily be seen to be intimately related to adverbial modifications. Consider the compound sentence 'If the house is gray and being gray is dull then there is something dull about the house'. The expression 'being gray' can be viewed as the product of a nominalizing transformation of the predicate adjective 'gray'. By such an operation, the expression is converted to a noun phrase and thus rendered available for predication. If we try to indicate, in the notation of quantificational logic, the structure of such a sentence, we seem compelled to conjure up a special entity, the abstract entity supposedly denoted by the expression 'being gray'. For it clearly will not do to translate the sentence as '$(x)[Hx$. Gx .$\supset$. $Dx]$', where 'Hx' stands in place of 'x is a house', 'Gx' in place of 'x is gray', and 'Dx' in place of 'x is dull'. That is not what we were saying: there may be something dull about the house even though the house is not dull.

Here it may be said that since the English sentence seems to say something about an abstract entity, the property of being gray, there is no reason to balk at a translation of the sentence that employs quantifications over predicate letters, or that calls for properties as values of its variables. But there is no good reason to suppose that the English sentence makes reference to any abstract entity. For there is no good reason to suppose that such a nominalization as 'being gray' must be construed as a referring expression. To say that being gray is dull is not to say that there is some entity, namely the property of being gray, and that entity is dull. To say that being gray is dull is to say that if anything is gray then, not it is dull *simpliciter* but, it is dull in respect of color, or it is dull to a certain degree, perhaps a slight and discountable degree, or it is somewhat or partially dull. And here evidently these various prepositional phrases all play the role of adverbial modifiers.

Again, consider the sentence 'Tardiness is reprehensible': the word 'tardiness' can be viewed as the product of a distinct morphologically productive process, a nominalizing transformation of the predicate adjective 'tardy'. By affixing '-ness', the adjective 'tardy' is converted to a noun and thus rendered available for predication. To say that tardiness is reprehensible is again not to make reference to any supposed abstract entity: it is a way of saying, not that if anyone is tardy then he is reprehensible, which would be somewhat harsh, but rather that if anyone is tardy then he is *prima facie* reprehensible, which is compatible with not being reprehensible at all, for he may have an excuse that gets him off. And again here one is evidently dealing with an adverbial modification.

Quine has said "To paraphrase a sentence into the canonical notation of quantification is, first and foremost, to make its ontic content explicit, quantification being a device for talking in general of objects". And he has said that "To decline to explain oneself in terms of quantification, or in terms of those special idioms of ordinary language by which quantification is directly explained, is simply to decline to disclose one's referential intent".[9] But I conclude that the invitation to produce such a paraphrase is a gambit to be played with considerable care and, on occasion, to be declined.

A quantificational logic is a remarkably rigid device for

[9] Willard V. O. Quine, *Word and Object* (Cambridge: Technology Press, 1960) 242, 243.

plotting our discourse in terms of what can be said about discrete objects. It stands to English as a Mercator projection does to a globe; it is not better, but perhaps not worse, than that. If one is to represent the various sentences of English in a quantificational logic then inevitably one is compelled to perform feats of conjuration, to produce abstract and special entities. And that may be not a matter of making "ontic content explicit" but unhappily of creating the illusion of content. For there is no good reason to credit the existence of such entities apart from the particular system of logic which evokes them. They are best seen as devices, devised to flatten the path from the sphere of natural language to the plane of logic: not entities from some Platonic realm of being, but simply isoglosses drawn by a logistic cartographer concerned to plot a plausible course through our conceptual labyrinth.

IV

Natural and
Formal Languages

That a formal logic is itself a language, of a sort, is today a common view. The articulation of such a view may rightly be considered one of the significant achievements of contemporary logical and linguistic research. But there is a posture from which formal logic is seen not merely as a language of a sort but as the ideal and proper form of language, the exemplar to which those evolutionary products that we call "natural languages" constitute at best abortive approximations. So viewed, a natural language, such as English, cannot help but take on a bad ambiguous topsy-turvy look. This world will, after all, look upside down if one stands on one's head.

Characteristically a formal language is constituted by a precisely specifiable set of expressions and various perfectly precise rules for their manipulation, combination and interpretation. In consequence, in contrast with any natural language, a formal logic and formal languages in general appear to have the undeniable virtues of precision and clarity. But these virtues are purchased at a cost: the cost is the utter inutility of the formal language as a language with which to communicate in the world in which we find ourselves.

Characteristically the use of language calls for a physical transaction between distinct complexly structured organisms in a complexly structured context. I prefer to think and shall here speak of speakers and hearers as automata of a sort (organic rather than mechanical). The speaker-automaton puts out a certain set of linguistic data which is transmitted acoustically to the hearer. Some subset of the data is then received by and constitutes an input to the hearer-automaton. Generally the hearer will receive other sensory inputs at the same time. The input data is then processed in some way in accordance with the program, state and structure of the hearer.

The realities of this complex linguistic transaction go and must go unheeded, ignored, if one is to dwell in the somewhat mythic and certainly myopic reaches of a formalism.

To begin with, the familiar forms of formal logic and formal languages are not equipped to cope with noise. And in the presence of noise the much vaunted absolute precision of a formal logic is apt to prove illusory. Yet in this world there is always noise.

The requirement that a formal language be perfectly precise can be and usually is expressed in terms of "effectiveness". For example, it is usually required that the rules and expressions of a formal language be such that the definition of a well-formed formula be effective in the sense that "there is a method by which, whenever a formula is given, it can always be determined effectively whether or not it is well-formed." [1] Effectiveness can be

[1] Alonzo Church, *Introduction to Mathematical Logic* (Princeton: Princeton University Press, 1956) 51.

construed in terms of there being an algorithm or a method of computation for determining whether or not something is so. To say, for example, that the specification of well-formedness is effective is to say that there is an algorithm or a method of computation for determining whether or not a given expression is a well-formed expression of the language.

But the existence of an algorithm neither confers certainty nor guarantees absolute precision.[2] Consider, in particular, the difficulty of determining whether or not an expression formed by the combination of several million symbols is a well-formed expression of the language. The existence of an algorithm merely guarantees that there is a method of computation. But it is still necessary to perform the computation if one is to determine whether or not the expression is well-formed. Unfortunately even the best of computers is, in the final analysis, fallible, as is anyone else. The reason is of course that any physical signal is subject to distortion, owing to noise or error or some sort of disturbance or failure in transmission: noise-free error-proof channels of communication are not to be had. The question whether or not an expression formed by the combination of several million symbols is a well-formed expression of the language in fact admits of only a probabilistic sort of answer.

Problems of distortion, noise, error and the like are generally ruled out by assumption in the specification of a formal language.[3] However, von Neumann's probabilistic logic provides an example of a formal language devised to cope with problems occasioned by a failure of transmis-

[2] See Church, *op. cit.*, 53, for what appears to be a contrary view.
[3] See Church, *op. cit.*, 51.

sion.[4] Such a system, in contrast with more familiar logics, thus constitutes a somewhat more perspicuous representation of an actual language.

In contrast with the familiar forms of formal language, a natural language, such as English, is and is bound to be distinctly noise-oriented. The realities of a linguistic transaction are such that a successful use of language to communicate is possible only if a variety of strategies is available.

Redundancy is the principal device for coping with noise, transmission failures and the like. But redundancy has many forms. The utterance uttered by a speaker in the course of a speech transaction may itself be redundant; thus the plural affix '-s' is redundant in 'He has eight books.' This sort of redundancy constitutes a form of multiplexing and is available in connection with formal languages and computing machinery. But there is another form of redundancy frequently to be encountered in actual linguistic transactions and this form is not available in connection with formal languages or with computing machinery not programmed for pattern recognition.

Consider a speaker and a hearer both of whom are seated together at a dinner table; the speaker, holding up a piece of bread, turns to the hearer and says 'This bread tastes terrible.' A redundant aspect of this transaction is to be seen in the fact that, in that context, the speaker probably would have communicated the same information if in

---

[4] See John von Neumann, "Probabilistic Logics and the Synthesis of Reliable Organisms from Unreliable Components," in C. E. Shannon and J. McCarthy, eds., *Automata Studies* (Princeton: Princeton University Press, 1956) 43–98.

fact he had said 'This bed tastes terrible': the phonemic contrast between 'bed' and 'bread' is rendered redundant by the perceptual features of the situation.

More generally, in the actual use of language the relevant inputs to the hearer need not be simply those corresponding to the linguistic output of the speaker during the course of the particular linguistic transaction. In particular, speakers often supply, or rely on the fact that the hearer is supplied with, various visual data.

Formal languages ignore the realities of the perceptual situation in a wholehearted manner: not only do they make no concession to the existence of perceptual difficulties, they eschew all reliance on perceptual strategies and abilities. But such reliance is characteristic of the use of a natural language and successful communication would be virtually impossible without it.

Consider the singular descriptive phrase employed as subject of the sentence 'The pen on the desk is made of gold'. By the use of such a phrase in an appropriately structured context one may well succeed in singling out a unique referent even though of course the English phrase 'the pen on the desk' does not have a unique referent. But from a purely formal point of view, a use of the phrase 'the pen on the desk' is to be deplored: since the expression does not in fact have a unique referent, the sentence 'The pen on the desk is made of gold' is formally classed either true, or false, or neither true nor false, depending on the system in question.

It is sometimes supposed that one could avoid the use of such phrases by making explicit what is merely implicit in the context of utterance.[5] But that is not true. For example, instead of the short phrase 'the pen on the desk', one could perhaps find a long elaborate descriptive phrase presumably referring to the same referent, say, 'the pen on the desk in the study of the house at 3415 Black Hawk Drive in Madison, Wisconsin, at 8:00 A.M. on January 26, 1968'. But such a phrase does not make explicit what was merely implicit in the context. For no conning of the context of utterance enables one to glean the information that the house in question was located in Madison, Wisconsin, that the date was January 26, and so on. Furthermore, there is no way in which the factors serving to render the use of the short phrase efficacious in context can be made explicit. The hearer who understands what is said and who can determine what the referent of the phrase is does so by relying not simply on supplementary information but on the exercise of all sorts of perceptual and conceptual strategies. In particular, an exercise of the abilities required for pattern recognition is obviously called for.

To employ the long descriptive phrase rather than the more familiar short one would not be a matter of making explicit what was only implicit. Neither could it in any sense be said to exemplify an increase in precision. If anything, a use of the formally preferred long phrase would, in the actual use of language, contribute to imprecision, vagueness and uncertainty since it would undoubtedly serve to increase the probability of error: seeing the gold-colored pen on the desk before him, the hearer need have

[5] See Willard V. O. Quine, *Word and Object* (Cambridge: Technology Press, 1960) 183.

no difficulty in locating the referent of the phrase; but what the date is is apt to be a matter for conjecture.

For a speaker to supply or rely on nonlinguistic inputs to the hearer is a commonplace in the use of a natural language. It is equally commonplace and equally essential for a speaker to be able, on occasion, to rely on a hearer's having a special program. The distinction between input data and a program is not a formal distinction: the program is simply data that serve to define a function to be computed by the automaton. In consequence, if a speaker wishes to minimize reliance on the program of the hearer, he can put out a more explicit linguistic datum. Conversely, if greater reliance on the program of the hearer is feasible and desirable, the speaker's linguistic output can be considerably compressed.

In all discourse, save that in which the speaker is attempting to communicate with a hearer that the speaker believes not to understand the language, the speaker relies on the hearer's having a specific linguistic program peculiar to the persons who speak or understand the language in which the discourse takes place. But speakers generally rely on the hearer's having a further special program as well, where this special program corresponds to specific information, knowledge, beliefs and so forth pertaining to nonlinguistic matters. For example, relying on the fact that the hearer knows that alligators do not wear shoes, a speaker may say 'I bought a pair of alligator shoes' and expect to be understood. Again, a speaker may say 'I saw a man trying to stand on his head' and expect to be understood as saying that he viewed a man who was attempting a headstand, not that he uses a saw on people and not that the man in question was attempting to decapitate himself and then stand on the decapitated head. (Possibly the compound 'alligator shoes' may be held to have a special linguistic structure that serves to block the reading 'shoes worn by alligators', but the other sentence would certainly be ambiguous were it not for the hearer's special program. There is no sharp line to be drawn between the specifically linguistic program and the special nonlinguistic program of a person who understands a particular dialect.)

From a purely formal point of view, a speaker's reliance on a hearer's special program is to be anathematized in so far as it sanctions implicit rather than explicit qualification. Consider a situation in which a doorkeeper of a theatre after a performance reports to the manager 'No one got in without a ticket'; implicit to this discourse is the qualification that employees and players are not in question. The doorkeeper is not saying that no person whatever, including himself, who entered the theatre did so without a ticket. From a formal point of view, the more explicit report 'No one, other than employees and players, got in without a ticket' would appear preferable to the implicitly qualified 'No one got in without a ticket'. But in fact, the explicit qualification would serve no purpose in the linguistic transaction we are supposing to have occurred; the explicit qualification would neither facilitate communication nor increase precision. On the contrary, discourse would tend to break down under the strain of explicitness. It is not merely that the resulting prolixity would be aesthetically unbearable: there would be a general failure of communication.

Consider, for example, the plight of an officer who wishes to order a private to shut a door. He might say to the private 'Shut the door!'. The private then replies 'Yes, sir' and does nothing. The officer might then resort to the more explicit 'Shut the door now!', whereupon the private shuts the door for a second and then opens it as it was. For he was not told to shut the door and leave it shut. And if he were told to shut it and leave it shut, there would then be the question how long was he to leave it shut? Or consider the maze one maunders in in attempting to make explicit the simple request 'Please tell me the time'. Where? Here. When? Now. According to what standard. Eastern Standard Time. With what tolerance? Plus or minus two seconds. In what language? English. What dialect? East Coast American. In how loud a voice? How quickly? (Yet if we are ever to make a conversational robot we shall have to make our way through such a maze as this.)

That speakers characteristically rely on hearers' having special programs is of a piece with the fact that communication is characteristically an intramural affair and fares badly when cultural lines are crossed. And it is in the reliance on special programs that the different dialects of a natural language have their provenance.

In the use of language a speaker may rely on the hearer's receiving nonlinguistic inputs and on the hearer's having a specific program and structure. But the speaker's principal resources are to be found in his own program and structure. To speak one must use words (or their equivalents) and so the speaker must have or must find words to use: he must have some sort of vocabulary. The profound differences between a formal language and a natural language take their loci in the respective vocabularies of each language.

A vocabulary may be thought of as constituted by a finite explicit store of words together with a set (possibly null) of morphologically productive devices. Consider a formal language, the words of which are 'x', 'x'', 'x''', . . . , thus an infinite number of words. The vocabulary of this language is then constituted by an explicit store of one word, 'x', and a recursive device for the further production of infinitely many words; thus the language has an explicit store of one word, an implicit store of infinitely many.

For the sake of definiteness, consider not the English language, which is as it were a vast slow perhaps soon to be completed process, the vocabulary of which obviously cannot conceivably be effectively specified, but rather the speech of a single speaker at a moment of time, say some person's idiolect here and now. The vocabulary of this speaker can then be identified with products of morphologically productive operations over some explicit store of words.

(The processes of lexical production are enormously varied complex and variously operative. Some productive lexical processes are virtually uniform throughout the language, for example, those by which plurals, past tenses, the familiar inflectional forms, are formed. Some processes are only fairly regular, for example, that process by which a set of adverbs can be produced from a set of adjectives by suffixing '-ly' ('quickly' from 'quick'). Another fairly regular production is exemplified by an operation over a domain of adjectives which consists in suffixing '-ish' and producing an adjective. The operation over 'green' yields 'greenish', and over 'greenish', 'greenishish', and so on. Or consider a pair of operations, one being that of suffixing '-ness' to an adjective yielding a noun, the other being that of suffixing '-ish' to a noun yielding an adjective. This pair of operations then produces 'quickness', "quickness-ish', 'quicknessishness', and so on. (Although operations yielding infinite sets of products may seem somewhat counterintuitive and certainly produce lexical curiosities, there is no need to be excessively squeamishish about the matter. Contemporary transformational grammar has analogous progeny, as for example, 'The old old old old old old old old old old old problem is ever with us'.) Some productive lexical processes appear to have a more limited scope. The operation of suffixing '-er' to a verb to form a noun ('walker' from 'walk') is of considerable importance though one does not have 'fatherer' from 'father', 'rainer' from 'rain,' 'horser' from 'horse', and in fact, 'peddle' is a back-formation from 'peddler'. And then there are such limited processes as those that have given rise to 'beatnik,' 'peacenik', 'noodnik', to 'telethon', 'sellathon', to "cinerama', 'Christorama', and so on.)

The vocabulary of a formal language may be either finite or infinite. In either case the vocabulary of a formal language is effectively specifiable. In contrast, no nonarbitrary specification of the vocabulary of a natural language, or dialect, or idiolect can possibly be effective.

Presumably a word is in the vocabulary of a person at a fixed moment of time if and only if, at that time, first, he is able to use it correctly, given appropriate conditions for doing so, and secondly, an inability to understand a sentence in which the word is used is not attributable to a difficulty with the word in question. (The second condition has been invoked here to rule out the following sort of case: a person may be able to use the word 'buccal' correctly in that if he were presented with a substance indentified as "hirudin", he could rightly say of it 'It is an anticoagulant extracted from the buccal glands of a leech'. But he need not be able to understand the question 'Are they buccal?' asked in reference to certain glands, and this inability could be directly attributable to his not knowing what 'buccal' means. In consequence, in accordance with the second condition, 'buccal' could not be classed a word in his vocabulary. If, however, one wished to insist that even so 'buccal' is a word of his vocabulary, the second condition could simply be deleted.)

The specification just provided of a persons's vocabulary at a fixed moment of time is clearly not effective in any plausible sense of the word. There neither is nor does it even seem plausible to suppose there could be any sort of algorithm for determining either which words a person is able to use correctly or when an inability to understand a sentence in which the word is used is attributable to a difficulty with the word.

One might suppose that a way of determining whether or not the first condition is satisfied is as follows: take a biggish lexicon, say *Webster's Third International*; with respect to each word, test to see if the person is able to use it correctly. First, unfortunately and without a doubt there will be words of his vocabulary that are not in that dictionary: 'peacenik', 'hippy', 'greenishish', 'squint-eyedishness'. Second one finds that under such test conditions a person may fail to identify words that, given an appropriate occasion for use, he would use unhesitatingly and with ease. That it is not possible to specify a person's vocabulary effectively is hardly surprising when one realizes that no one, not even the speaker himself, has altogether free access to his vocabulary.

Think of a speaker as an automaton and of his vocabulary as a partially implicit and partially explicit store of words (the implicit store being that derivable by morphologically productive techniques): an educated speaker of English is bound to have a remarkably large and varied explicit store of words. In consequence there are bound to be remarkably complex storage arrangements serving to ensure reasonably adequate access to storage.

Perhaps the most inscrutable aspect of an ordinary person's ability to use words is displayed in the ease and swiftness with which he finds the words to use: an ordinary speaker is a word-finding device *par excellence*. Ask him to describe the scene before him and at once the right words flow forth. Evidently given an appropriate occasion for use he has almost instant access to storage. Ready access to storage given an appropriate occasion for use is of course required if one is to speak a language with ease. But there is no reason at all to suppose that there either is or should be free and ready access to storage apart from an appropriate context and cues. What purpose would it serve? (But of course people differ with respect to ease of access, which is part of the reason why some are better than others at doing crossword puzzles.)

In considering the vocabulary of a speaker what are important, however, are not just the words he is able to use but rather what I propose to speak of as the "word-senses" that he is able to use. If two speakers both use the verb 'cool', but the first uses the word in two senses ('Cool the meat' and 'Cool it man!') While the second uses it in only one, then in a important sense the first speaker has a larger vocabulary then the second. I shall say that the first speaker has (so far) a vocabulary of two word-senses, the second only one.

That no one has altogether free access to word storage is only one reason why it is not in fact possible to provide a nonarbitrary effective specification of a speaker's vocabulary The fact of the matter is that a natural language (or dialect or idiolect) does not have a store of words or word-senses. The words or word-senses of a natural language do not constitute a set in the set-theoretic sense of 'set.' The vocabulary of words and word-senses of a natural language is a continuous creation.

The expressions of a formal language are character-istically required to be monosemous to comply with the general requirements of effectiveness. In contrast, polysemy is a characteristic feature of any natural language. For example, with respect to a standard moderate sized dictionary such as *Webster's Seventh New Collegiate,* an educated guess would be that of the 70,000 entries listed, at least 20,000 have at least three reasonably distinct meanings and thus are triply polysemous. *Webster's Seventh Collegiate* is then a lexicon of 70,000 words but of at least 110,000 word-senses.

From the point of view of a formalism, polysemy can be seen only as a cancerous proliferation of meanings, calling for swift excision. The operation could be performed but nothing would be accomplished thereby; the proliferation would inevitably continue and, what is worse, there would be an immediate price to pay for the surgical insult. To eliminate even the evident homonymy and polysemy from a lexicon of a natural language would mean at least doubling the number of entires. And this would mean an enormous increase in the probability of error in the transmission and reception of signals. For instead of n phonemic patterns to be stored and rendered available for the appropriate processing, $2n$ such patterns would have to be so dealt with.

Though polysemy and homonymy can give rise to ambiguity in the use of words, by and large the ambiguity is merely potential. Syntactic, discourse and contextual factors all serve as effective palliatives. There is no ambiguity of the sentence 'I can't bear to live with a bear in the house' that is attributable to the word 'bear' despite the fact that the word is both homonymous and polysemous. Here syntactic and discourse factors suffice to preclude an ambiguity. 'Put it on the table' is not apt to be ambiguous in the appropriate perceptual situation despite the fact that 'table' is disinctly polysemous. Again, there is not apt to be anything ambiguous about 'He just refused that dish' when said of a workman standing in front of the fusebox of a paraboloid microwave antenna. Reliance on a plurality of factors is the rule, not the exception, in the everyday use of language. But even if polysemy were the plague, there is nothing for it: it is an inevitable by-product of the successful use of words to communicate with in the sort of world we are in.

As I have elsewhere maintained,[6] a word's having meaning in a language can be thought of in terms of the word's having associated with it a set of conditions, where a condition is taken to be that which is expressed by an open

[6] *Semantic Analysis* (Ithaca: Cornell University Press, 1960) 171 ff.

sentence, a predicative expression, or that which can be explicitly stated by employing a nominalized predicative expression. For example, the word 'brother' has associated with it (at least) the two conditions of being male and of being a sibling. But owing to the complex character of the contexts in which words are used and the purposes for which they are used, one finds that inevitably the set of conditions associated with a word is subject to constant variation. The continual modulation of meaning is characteristic of all discourse in a natural language.

If the set of conditions associated with a word admits of a reasonably clear bifurcation into two virtually exclusive proper subsets, such that in the contexts in which the word is used the members of either one subset or the other are relevant but not both, then the word is polysemous having at least two relatively distinct meanings. For example, the word 'division' has associated with it a subset of conditions pertaining to army groups and a subset of conditions pertaining to arithmetic matters. Although there are cases in which 'division' is used such that both subsets of conditions are relevant, such cases are rare and such a use of the word takes on the character of a pun, as in 'I want to see Lt. George's division' meaning both his army group and his arithmetic.

If the set of conditions associated with a word does not admit of any clear bifurcation into exclusive subsets, it may still be the case that in certain contexts only certain proper subsets are in fact relevant. If so, such a word is not polysemous in that it does not have distinct meanings, but it is akin to a polysemous word in that it has a plurality of senses. For example, the word 'brother' has associated with it not only the conditions of being male and of being a sibling but also the condition of behaving fraternally. The first two are but the third is not relevant in connection with the utterance 'Does he have a brother?', whereas the third is but the first two are not relevant in connection with the utterance 'He has been a brother to me'. On the other hand, there are unpunlike common cases in which all three conditions are relevant, as in 'I wish I had a brother'.

Neither polysemy nor a plurality of senses need be confused with generality, though the distinction is subtle. I can here do no more than indicate the direction in which the distinction is made. The word 'tiger', for example, has associated with it the condition of being striped. Should one encounter a creature *sans* stripes, one could nonetheless characterize it as "a tiger", albeit a freakish one. In so doing, one need not be using the word 'tiger' in a special sense. The difference between this sort of case and the cases of the distinct senses of 'brother' is related to the fact that the condition of being striped is relevant in connection with the question 'Is that a tiger?' even if it should prove to be the case that the condition is not satisfied, whereas the condition of being a sibling is irrelevant in connection with the question 'Has he been a brother to you?'.

One can distinguish between polysemy and a plurality of senses and generality but only as one can distinguish between segments of a varying continuum, a constantly shifting spectrum. For the sets of conditions associated with the words of a natural language do not stay put. They could if the world would but it won't and so they don't.

I can supply no effective catalogue of the means of modulating the meaning of words. But some of the ways are obvious and familiar. One uses a word in a restricted sense when one wishes to slough off unwanted conditions. To restrict the set of conditions is to put what Empson has called "a depreciative pregnancy" on the word.[7] One can also use a word in an expanded sense; when Hamlet said of his father 'He was a man', he was putting "an appreciative pregnancy" on 'man', thus adding the condition of being courageous to the set associated with 'man'. A use of a word in a shifted sense occurs when one speaks of "baking bread" for of course one bakes dough which becomes bread on the completion of the process (just so 'digging a ditch', 'winning a race', 'building a house'). When a novel set of conditions is associated with a word only for the immediate occasion of use, the word is said to have "a nonce sense". And then there are such classical devices as irony, metaphor, metonymy and so forth.

The inevitable upshot of the constant modulation of meaning under the pressures of usage is the appearance of polysemy in a language. Owing to the nature of the phenomena dealt with, the use of a word in a natural language must take on something of the character of an operation with an analogue device. In contrast, the vocabulary of a formal language can readily be digital in character.

One could attempt to abort the birth of polysemy in a natural language by expanding the language's explicit vocabulary as follows. First, if a word w_0 has a set of conditions a associated with it, and a has n elements, then form the power set of a, call it 'P'; w_0 may then be dropped from the vocabulary of the language and replaced by distinct words w_1, w_2, . . . , w_2n where to each w_i there corresponds one and only one element of P (excluding the null set). Thus there will be no occasion ever to restrict the

[7] William Empson, *The Structure of Complex Words* (New York: New Directions, n.d.).

sense of any word. However, this will still not account for the use of a word with an expanded sense, or in a shifted sense or in a novel sense. Hence second, we shall have to find some means of constructing a complete vocabulary so as to obviate the need for expanding and shifting and creating senses. There is excellent reason to suppose that neither of these steps is at all feasible.

Consider, for example, the sentence 'It was a fine drive' and the various matters that may be in question: a backhand drive in tennis, a drive in the country, a cattle drive, the army's drive on the eastern front, sexual drive, the garage drive. *Webster's Seventh Collegiate* implausibly lists some 40 senses of 'drive'. One may plausibly suppose that anyway at least 6 conditions can be associated with the word. Were one then to introduce a separate word for each combination of conditions according to the indicated formula one would have to introduce 63 distinct words to replace the single word 'drive'. It should be evident at once that the cure for polysemy would be worse than the disease. For how could one store the resultant prodigious number of words in such a way as to ensure reasonably adequate access to storage? (The problem here is analogous to that one would encounter were one to attempt to replace a useful analogue device such as a slide rule with a digital device such as a table of correlations corresponding to all discriminable positions of the slide on the body.) The enormous utility of a single word's having a plurality of senses is to be seen in the fact that the word then constitutes a coding device serving to ensure reasonable access to the stored plurality of senses. (Although all formal languages in fact rely heavily on coding devices and would be utterly unintelligible without them, the devices, namely abbreviative definitions, are officially disclaimed and denied formal status.)

A complete vocabulary, in the sense intended here, would be one that obviated the need for further modulating the meaning of words. It would comprise all the words anyone could ever devise. But the question whether a given vocabuulary is so complete makes sense only if one could effectively enumerate all possible conditions that a human being could conceive of as obtaining in the universe. Whether this is possible would appear to depend on the neurophysiological structure of the human brain. If its structure were analyzable in terms of discrete states, perhaps such an enumeration could be effected. But there appears to be little reason to suppose that the brain is so analyzable.

Formal logics and formal languages are bright shiny conceptual instruments of great beauty and precision. They permit of operations more delicate than could be performed by even the finest surgical laser. But they are unsuitable for use as languages to communicate with in this world. Being bound to the requirements of effectiveness, they are bound to lose lustre when exposed to the corrosive forces of actual discourse.

In discussing the requirements of effectiveness Church has said: "The requirements of effectiveness are (of course) not meant in the sense that a structure which is analogous to a logistic system except that it fails to satisfy these requirements may not be useful for some purposes or that it is forbidden to consider such—but only that a structure of this kind is unsuitable for use or interpretation as a language. For, however indefinite or imprecisely fixed the common idea of a language may be, it is at least fundamental to it that a language shall serve the purpose of communication. And to the extent that requirements of effectiveness fail, the purpose of communication is defeated." [8] English fares badly on this account. For the requirements of effectiveness are flaunted by a natural language and in every quarter. There is no algorithm for determining which expressions are well-formed and which are not. There is no algorithm for determining which expressions are words of the language and which are not. In the set-theoretic sense of 'set', there is no such thing as the set of English expressions or the set of English words. And when one speaks in English or in any natural language there is always room for conjecture whether one has managed to communicate anything at all.

If Church is right and I am right too then perhaps nothing is suitable for use as a language. But that is no reason to quit talking: we are all going to do that anyway.

[8] *Op. cit.*, 52.

V

On H. P. Grice's
Account of Meaning

Because I believe the coin is counterfeit, because it seems to be gaining currency, I mean to examine and attempt to discredit an account of meaning circulated some time ago by H. P. Grice.[1]

Those among us concerned with problems of semantics are much concerned with the sense(s) or meaning(s) of the morpheme 'mean' in (1) and (2):

(1) The sentence 'Snow is white' means snow is white.

(2) The adjective 'ungulate' means having hoofs.

Other senses or meanings of 'mean' are of interest in semantics primarily only in so far as they have some bearing on 'mean' in either (1) or (2).

Grice's paper is entitled "Meaning". It appears to be an account of meaning that is supposed to have some bearing on the senses of 'mean' in (1) and (2).

Grice apparently says that 'mean' in (1) and (2) is used in what he calls "nonnatural" senses of the verb. He uses the abbreviation 'mean-nn' to mark the "nonnatural" senses of 'mean'. He offers something of an analysis of 'mean-nn' (and of the morphological variants, 'meant-nn', 'means-nn', and so forth).

1 "Meaning," *The Philosophical Review* LXVI (1957) 377–388.

Does 'mean' in (1) or (2) have the sense(s) indicated by Grice's analysis?

It will simplify matters to adopt the following convention: when the expression 'mean-nn' (or any of its variants) is used here, that expression is to have the sense(s) indicated by and in conformance with Grice's analysis. The problem of this paper can then be stated in a simple way.

Consider (1nn) and (2nn):

(1nn) The sentence 'Snow is white' means-nn snow is white.

(2nn) The adjective 'ungulate' means-nn having hoofs.

Is (1nn) simply a restatement of (1), (2nn) of (2)?

After an ingenious intricate discussion, Grice arrives at the following "generalizations": [2]

(i) 'A meant-nn something by *x*' is (roughly) equivalent to 'A intended the utterance of *x* to produce some effect in an audience by means of the recognition of this intention'.

(ii) '*x* meant-nn something' is (roughly) equivalent to 'Somebody meant-nn something by *x*'.

(iii) '*x* means-nn (timeless) that so-and-so' might as a first shot be equated with some statement or disjunction of statements about what "people" (vague) intend (with qualifications about 'recognition') to effect by *x*.

It is indicated in the discussion that the letter 'A' is supposed to be replaceable by the name of a person, that the letter '*x*' may be but need not be replaced by a sentence.

[2] Page 385.

Thus it is evident that Grice's account is supposed to apply to sentence (1) and so to (1nn). Although he mentions words in the course of his discussion,[3] none of the "generalizations" appear to apply to words. Thus apparently he is not concerned to supply, in the paper in question, an account of the sense of 'mean' in (2). Consequently, I mean to forget about (2) and (2nn) and be concerned here only with (1) and (1nn).

Of the three "generalizations" stated, (iii) is the only one that directly applies to (1nn). Unfortunately, (iii) is not particularly pellucid. (Even so, what emerges from the fog will be sufficient to establish certain points.) Let us begin by examining (i) and (ii) in the hope of gaining insight into (iii).

On being inducted into the army, George is compelled to take a test designed to establish sanity. George is known to be an irritable academic. The test he is being given would be appropriate for morons. One of the questions asked is: 'What would you say if you were asked to identify yourself?'. George replied to the officer asking the question by uttering (3):

(3) Ugh ugh blugh blugh ugh blug blug.

According to the dictum of (i), George meant-nn something by (3): he intended the utterance of (3) to produce an effect in his audience by means of the recognition of his intention. The effect he intended was that of offending his audience. The accomplishment of this effect depended on the recognition of his intention. (The case in question is also in accordance with the various caveats

[3] Page 379.

noted by Grice in the course of his discussion: the officer testing George could "refuse to be offended", the intended effect thus being in some sense within the control of the audience; George's intention to offend was his "primary" intention; [4] and so forth.) Consequently, as far as one can tell, (3) fills Grice's bill.

But even though it is clear that George meant-nn something by (3), it is equally clear that George did not mean anything by (3). Grice seems to have conflated and confused 'A meant something by uttering x', which is true in a case like (3), with the quite different 'A meant something by x', which is untrue in a case like (3).

The malady just noted in connection with (i) of course at once infects (ii). For even though it is clear that George meant-nn something by (3) and hence (3) meant-nn something, it is equally clear that (3) did not mean anything. Indeed, had (3) meant anything, that would have defeated George's purpose in uttering (3).

The preceding case admits of the following variation. On being given the test over again by another officer, instead of uttering (3), George uttered (4):

(4) pi·hi·y pi·hi·y.

Again in accordance with (i) we can say that George meant-nn something by (4) and what he meant-nn was precisely what he meant-nn by (3). (For we may suppose that he had the same intention in each case, expected the same reaction, and so forth.)

But in this case, not only did George mean something by uttering (4), he also meant something by (4): even though

[4] Page 386.

he rightly expected his utterance to be treated as though it were mere noise, what he meant by (4), and what he said, was that he didn't know. George was perversely speaking in Hopi.[5] (Here one need not confuse 'George did not mean what he said', which is true, for he did know the answer to the question, with the quite different 'George did not mean anything by (4)', which is untrue.)

That George meant-nn something by (4) is wholly irrelevant to the question whether George meant something by (4). And the fact that (4) meant-nn something—in virtue of (ii)—is wholly irrelevant to the question whether (4) meant anything. This should be obvious from the fact that what (4) meant had nothing whatever to do with what George intended to effect by uttering the utterance and hence had nothing whatever to do with what (4) meant-nn.

The curious character of (ii) can be further displayed by the following sort of cases. Consider (5):

(5) Claudius murdered my father.

and let us conjure up three contexts of utterance: (a) George uttered a sentence token of type (5), thus he uttered (5a), in the course of a morning soliloquy; (b) George uttered another such token, (5b), in the afternoon in the course of a discussion with Josef; and (c) George uttered another such token, (5c), in the evening while delirious with fever. Now consider (6) and (6nn):

(6) (5a) meant the same as (5b) which meant the same as (5c) which meant the same as (5a).

[5] See Benjamin L. Whorf, *Language, Thought, and Reality* (Cambridge: Technology Press, 1956) 114, for the phonetic significance of (4).

where (6nn) is the same as (6) save that for each occurrence of 'meant' in (6), (6nn) has an occurrence of 'meant-nn'. Thus (6) says that the three tokens in question all had the same meaning; (6nn) says that they all had the same meaning-nn.

Although (6) is true, according to Grice's account, (6nn) must be false—here taking (6) and (6nn) to stand for statements. That this is so can be seen as follows.

According to (ii), a sentence S meant-nn something (roughly) if and only if somebody meant-nn something by it. Thus (5a), (5b), and (5c) meant-nn something (roughly) if and only if somebody meant-nn something by them.

Did anyone mean-nn anything by (5c)? Evidently not. For (5c) was uttered while George was delirious with fever, unaware of any audience. Hence (5c) was not intended to produce any effect in an audience. (Here one need not confuse 'What George said meant nothing', which may be true in one sense of 'what George said', with 'The expression which George uttered meant nothing', which is untrue.)

Did anyone mean-nn anything by (5b)? Presumably so. Since (5b) was uttered by George in the course of a discussion with Josef, if anything fits Grice's account, (5b) does.

Did anyone mean-nn anything by (5a)? It would seem not, for since George uttered (5a) in the course of a soliloquy, it could hardly have been intended to produce an effect in an audience. (But perhaps Grice would wish to maintain that, in so far as George was speaking to himself, he was his own audience. (But then could he intend to produce an effect in himself by means of a recognition on his own part of his own intention? These are mysteries we may cheerfully bequeath to Grice.))

Evidently (6nn) is untrue even though (6) is true.

Sentence token (5c) exemplifies a case in which even though it was not true that the speaker meant anything by the token, the token nonetheless meant something. One can also produce cases in which a speaker did mean something by an utterance and yet the utterance itself did not mean anything.

George has had his head tampered with: electrodes have been inserted, plates mounted, and so forth. The effect was curious: when asked how he felt, George replied by uttering (7):

(7) Glyting elly beleg.

What he meant by (7), he later informed us, was that he felt fine. He said that, at the time, he had somehow believed that (7) was synonymous with 'I feel fine' and that everyone knew this.

According to (i), George meant-nn something by (7), and according to (ii), (7) must have meant-nn something. But (7) did not mean anything at all.

The preceding examples should suffice to indicate that Grice's equivalences (i) and (ii) are untenable. But their extraordinary character can be made even plainer by the following sort of case.

A man suddenly cried out 'Gleeg gleeg gleeg!', intending thereby to produce a certain effect in an audience by means of the recognition of his intention. He wished to make his audience believe that it was snowing in Tibet. Of course he did not produce the effect he was after since no one recognized what his intention was. Nonetheless that he had such an intention became clear. Being deemed mad, he was turned over to a psychiatrist. He complained to the psychiatrist that when he cried 'Gleeg gleeg gleeg!' he had such an intention but no one recognized his intention and were they not mad not to do so.

According to Grice's equivalence (i), the madman meant-nn something by 'Gleeg gleeg gleeg!' and so, according to (ii), the madman's cry must have meant-nn something, presumably that it was snowing in Tibet. But the madman's cry did not mean anything at all; it certainly did not mean it was snowing in Tibet. Had it meant that, there would have been less reason to turn him over to a psychiatrist.

On Grice's account, good intentions suffice to convert nonsense to sense: the road to Babble is paved with such intentions.

It is time to turn to Grice's suggestion of an equivalence, (iii). Consider sentences (8), (9), and (9nn):

(8) He's a son of a stickleback fish.
(9) Sentence (9) means the male referred to is a son of a small scaleless fish (family Gasterosteidae) having two or more free spines in front of the dorsal fin.

where (9nn) is the same as (9) save that—as in (6nn)—'means' has given way to 'means-nn'.

I take it that there is no reason whatever to suppose that the sense of 'mean' in (9) differs in any way from the sense of 'mean' in (1). Both (9) and (1) are simply of the form:

sentence S means *m*. But if 'mean' in (9) has precisely the same sense as 'mean' in (1), it follows that (1nn) is not simply a restatement of (1). For (1) and (1nn) differ as (9) and (9nn) differ, and according to Grice's account, (9) and (9nn) are radically different. That this is so can be seen as follows.

I am inclined to suppose that (8) has been uttered only rarely. Nonetheless, taking (9) and (9nn) to stand for statements, I am reasonably certain that (9) is a reasonably correct statement of the meaning of (8) and I am being reasonable in being so certain.

If it is a correct statement of the meaning of (8), and if (9nn) is simply a restatement of (9), since (9nn) is, (9) must be equivalent to some statement or disjunction of statements about what "people" intend to effect by (8). So Grice evidently maintains; for despite its vagueness, that is what is indicated by (iii).

But the question 'What do people intend to effect by (8)?' would not be a sensible question. Since hardly anyone has ever uttered (8) before, or so I suppose, one can hardly ask what people intend to effect by it.

'Then what would people intend to effect by (8)?': the question is somewhat idle. What people would intend to effect by (8) is a matter about which one can only speculate, vaguely. However, since the obvious emendation of Grice's account invites such speculation, let us speculate.

What would people intend to effect by uttering (8)? Given the acoustic similarity between (8) and a familiar form of expression, given that sticklebacks are known to be tough fish, given that the sex of a fish is not readily determined by the uninitiated, most likely by uttering (8) people would thereby intend to denigrate a contextually indicated male person.

What people would intend to effect by (8) is a subject for profitless speculation. But if one must say something about the matter, I am inclined to suppose that (9nn) does not convey a correct account of what people would intend to effect by uttering (8). Thus (9nn) is presumably untrue.

If (9nn) were simply a restatement of (9), only a fool would profess to being even reasonably certain that (9) is a correct statement and it would be unreasonable of him to be so certain. But I am reasonably certain that (9) is a correct statement of the meaning of (8) and I am not being unreasonable in being so certain. Therefore (9nn)' cannot be simply a restatement of (9) and neither can (1nn) be simply a restatement of (1).

Before allowing Grice's analysis to rest in peace, the moral of its passing should be emphasized.

His suggestion is stated in terms of what people "intend", not in terms of what they "would intend". As such it obviously occasions difficulty with novel utterances. But matters are not at all improved by switching to what people "would intend".

For first, if a sentence is such that people in general simply would not utter it, then if they were to utter it, what they would intend to effect by uttering it might very well have nothing to do with the meaning of the sentence. What would a person intend to effect by uttering the sentence 'Snow is white and snow is white and snow is white and snow is white and snow is white'? I conjecture that a person uttering such a sentence could be a philosopher or a linguist or an avant-garde novelist or a child at play or a Chinese torturer. What people would intend to effect by uttering such a sentence would most likely have nothing whatever to do with the meaning of the sentence.

Secondly, the switch to 'would' would be of help only if there were a constructive method of determining what people would intend to effect by uttering an utterance. There is no such method. There is not likely to be any (at least in our lifetime).

Ignoring the futility of talking about what people "would intend" to effect by uttering an utterance, one need not ignore the fact that what people generally in fact mean may be altogether irrelevant to a meaning of an utterance.

By the spoken utterance 'HE GAVE HIM HELL' people generally mean what is meant by the written utterance 'He gave him hell' and not what is meant by the written utterance 'He gave him Hell'. Quite possibly no one has ever said 'I saw the children shooting' meaning by that he saws children while he is shooting. That is nonetheless one of the meanings of that remarkably ambiguous sentence. Indefinitely many such examples could be supplied.

To be concerned with what people intend (or would intend) to effect by uttering an expression is to be concerned with the use of the expression. As I have elsewhere pointed out and argued at length, the use of an expression is determined by many factors, many of which have nothing (or have nothing directly) to do with its meaning: acoustic shape is one such factor, length another.[6]

Grice's analysis rings untrue. It was bound to; his alloy

[6] *Semantic Analysis* (Ithaca: Cornell University Press, 1960).

lacks the basic ingredient of meaning—a set of projective devices. The syntactic and semantic structure of any natural language is essentially recursive in character. What any given sentence means depends on what (various) other sentences in the language mean.

That people generally intend (or would intend) this or that by uttering an utterance has, at best, as much significance as a statement to the effect that when 'Pass the salt!' is uttered, generally people are eating, thus what I have elsewhere called the statement of a "regularity".[7] Not all regularities are semantically relevant: a regularity couched in terms of people's "intentions" is not likely to be.

But even if such regularities were somehow relevant, that would not matter much. A regularity is no more than a ladder which one climbs and then kicks away. An account of meaning constituted by (i), (ii), and (iii) never gets off the ground. There is no reason to suppose it can.[8]

[7] *Op. cit.*
[8] I am indebted to Dennis Stampe for useful criticisms of various points.

VI

A Response to "Stimulus Meaning"

Presumably some words have some connection with something or other; and presumably it is in such connection that meaning takes its locus. But the character of that connection and of the elements connected has been a source of philosophic controversy. Some look for a relation between words and mental matters, images, the dubious intentions of speakers and so forth. Others try to connect words to behavior, words to deeds. Recently W. V. O. Quine has turned to his nerve endings: Quine looks to find the locus of meaning in the world pressing in on one's eyeballs.[1] More precisely, since, according to Quine and for reasons which need not concern us here, the common concept of meaning is a morass in which one need not maunder, to connect up some of our sentences with something in a world he has devised the concept of "stimulus meaning". I shall try to show that his peregrine proxy leads nowhere at all.

Quine preaches the primacy of the sentence in semantic theory:

[1] *Word and Object* (Cambridge: Technology Press, 1960). Subsequent parenthetic numerical references are to pages of this work.

Words can be learned as parts of longer sentences, and some words can be learned as one-word sentences through direct ostension of their objects. In either event, words mean only as their use in sentences is conditioned to sensory stimuli, verbal and otherwise. (9)

Any realistic theory of evidence must be inseparable from the psychology of stimulus and response, applied to sentences. (17)

He practices what he preaches: a stimulus meaning is the stimulus meaning of a sentence, and of that sentence for a speaker at a date (33). The stimulus meaning of a sentence S for a given speaker is definable in terms of the ordered pair of what he calls the "affirmative stimulus meaning" and the "negative stimulus meaning" of S for the given speaker (32). A stimulation σ belongs to the affirmative stimulus meaning of a sentence S for a given speaker if and only if there is a stimulation σ such that if the speaker were given σ', then were asked S, then were given σ, and then were asked S again, he would dissent the first time and assent the second. The negative stimulus meaning is defined similarly with 'assent' and 'dissent' interchanged, and the stimulus meaning is defined as the ordered pair of the two (32–33).

The stimulations to be gathered into the stimulus meaning of a sentence have temporal duration. A visual stimulation is identified with "the pattern of chromatic irradiation of the eye" (31), but the relevant stimulations are not "momentary irradiation patterns, but evolving irradiation patterns of all durations up to some convenient limit or *modulus*" (32). "Fully ticketed, therefore, a stimulus meaning is the stimulus meaning *modulo n* seconds of sentence S for speaker *a* at time *t*" (33).

To say that a speaker would assent to or dissent from a sentence *S* when supplied with appropriate stimulation is to speak in a "causal vein" (30). Quine is emphatic:

What now of that strong conditional, the 'would' in our definition of stimulus meaning? Its use here is no worse than its use when we explain '*x* is soluble in water' as meaning that *x* would dissolve if it were in water. What the strong conditional defines is a disposition, in this case a disposition to assent to or dissent from *S* when variously stimulated. (33)

To say that a speaker would assent to or dissent from a sentence S is then to say that the speaker has a disposition to assent to or dissent from *S* when variously stimulated. On Quine's view there is a causal connection between a stimulation and assent to or dissent from a sentence, when the speaker has a disposition to assent to or dissent from the sentence when variously stimulated: "the stimulation is what activates the disposition" (34).

Stimulus meaning is defined in terms of what a speaker would assent to or dissent from and thus, Quine says, in terms of the dispositions of the speaker. "The stimulus meaning of a sentence for a subject sums up his disposition to assent to or dissent from the sentence in response to present stimulation" (34). Quine is relatively explicit with respect to what he intends by the term 'disposition':

Dispositions are, . . . , a better-behaved lot than the general run of subjunctive conditionals; and the reason is that they are conceived as built-in, enduring structural traits. Their saving grace extends, moreover, to many subjunctive conditionals that do not happen to have acquired one-word tags like 'soluble' and 'fragile'. An example was the 'would prompt assent' of §8 (33). For there again a disposition was concerned, albeit unnamed:

some subtle neural condition, induced by language-learning, that disposes the subject to assent to or dissent from a certain sentence in response to certain supporting stimulations. (223)

Quine's conceptual apparatus can be paraded in the following play entitled "Tiger, anyone?". The script calls for a linguist, L, a Martian, who is concerned to effect a "radical translation" of a language, namely English, spoken by a native speaker, K. A "radical translation" is a "translation of the language of a hitherto untouched people" (28). For that purpose L has put a blindfold on K, for, we are told, "we may think of the ideal experimental situation as one in which the desired ocular exposure concerned is preceded and followed by a blindfold" (32). Awaiting ocular exposure immediately before K is a jungle tableau, tableau-I *sans* tiger. According to the book, the following events now occur: K's blindfold is removed by L; K's eyes are turned in the direction of tableau-I; his eyes are irradiated for a second or so and so he receives a nontiger-presenting stimulation; this nontiger-presenting stimulation activates a disposition to dissent from the sentence 'Tiger?' (32); the query 'Tiger?' is then put to K by L; this elicits a dissent from K, which is to say that "the prompting stimulation plus the ensuing query" (30) elicits K's dissent, a shake of the head or an equivalent; K's blindfold is restored; the curtain falls for a moment to rise anew on jungle tableau-II, one with a tiger; again K's blindfold is removed by L; K's eyes are turned in the direction of tableau-II; he receives a tiger-presenting stimulation; this tiger-presenting stimulation activates a disposition to assent to the sentence 'Tiger?'; the query 'Tiger?' is then put to K by L; the combination of prompting stimulation and ensuing query elicits an assent from K; K's blind-fold is restored and the curtain falls on the final scene of "Tiger, anyone?".

The plot is simple: the hero L is to establish that the tiger-presenting stimulation K received when confronted with tableau—II belonged to the affirmative stimulus meaning of 'Tiger?' for K at that time. Though the plot is simple, the play is a true flight of fancy standing squarely in the mainstream of romantic behaviorism.

Much in Quine's account makes one wonder, but the foremost fanciful feature is found in the assumption that speakers have dispositions to assent to or dissent from sentences. Even odder, in his account for any sentence a speaker assents to or dissents from, there is a corresponding disposition of the speaker. Stimulus meaning is, as we have seen and are told, defined in terms of a "strong conditional 'would' ", explicable in terms of dispositions to assent to or dissent from sentences. Hence for any sentence that has a stimulus meaning for a given speaker, there must be a corresponding disposition of that speaker and, Quine says, even such a sentence as 'There is ether drift' has a stimulus meaning (36) and so, presumably, virtually all declaratives have a stimulus meaning. (It is indicated that the concept of stimulus meaning is not as important in connection with a sentence like 'There is ether drift' as it is in connection with 'Tiger?' (36–37) but that is not to deny that the former has a stimulus meaning.)

Do speakers have dispositions to assent to or dissent from sentences? One would suppose that if dispositions are conceived as built-in, enduring structural traits, and Quine says so though I would not, then their number, with respect to a given individual, must be modest, plentiful perhaps as blackberries but not as grains of sand. But then there is the following sort of case.

Native speaker K is prevailed upon to view a sequence of tableaus: in the first, the numeral '1' is clearly displayed on a placard; in the second, the numeral '2' is so displayed; and so on for n tableaus. Of course n cannot become too large for, if it did, the condition that the numerals be clearly displayed could not be satisfied; and then there is the length of K's life to consider, not to mention his patience; yet n could conceivably reach the millions. For each i, in the i-th case a query of the form 'The numeral i?' is put to K and K assents, and for each i, in the i-th case a query of the form 'The numeral i-1?' is put to K and he dissents. Evidently, on Quine's account, K must have a disposition to assent to or dissent from 'The numeral '1'?', another different disposition to assent to or dissent from 'The numeral '2'?', and so on for some very large n. And then there is this question: if, having learned the language, K has a disposition to assent to or dissent from 'Salt?' when variously stimulated, and another disposition in connection with 'Bread?', must he have a further disposition in connection with 'Bread and salt?'? The proliferation of dispositions in the course of language learning would proceed at an appalling pace. But why suppose it?

There is no more reason to do so than there is to suppose that, for each problem it can cope with, a computer must somehow have a distinct corresponding structural feature. Perhaps one should pass this point. Without worrying overmuch about what it might mean, one might say that if a speaker has an "explicit" disposition in connection with 'Bread?' and another in connection with 'Salt?', then possibly he has an "implicit" disposition in connection with 'Bread and salt?'. And though it would be curious to speak of an "implicit structural trait", one could learn to live with it were there a reason to do so.

But even if one were now disposed to suppose that dispositions ("implicit" or "explicit") teemed in sufficient numbers, still it would be difficult to be responsive to the claim that "the stimulation is what activates the disposition" (34). At this moment, as at most, my visual stimulation is a nonzebu-presenting stimulation. If, as Quine says, the stimulation is what activates the disposition then at this moment, as at most, I must have an activated disposition to dissent from the query 'Zebu?'. But my present stimulation is not only a nonzebu-presenting stimulation, it is also a nonaardvark-presenting stimulation and a nonaardwolf and a nonabalone-presenting stimulation, and so on; and here of course, *ad infinitum*, for my present stimulation is not only a nonsingle-zebu-presenting stimulation, it is also a nonpair-of-zebus-presenting stimulation, and so on. So I also have an activated disposition to dissent from 'Aardvark?', 'Aardwolf?', 'Abalone?', 'Pair of zebus?', and so on.

Let us not, however, hastily assume that speakers of a language must essentially be dissentful on Quine's account since, on his account, on present stimulation any speaker is having activated dispositions to dissent from infinitely many queries. For, on Quine's account, any speaker on present stimulation is also having activated dispositions to assent to infinitely many queries: since my present stimulation is a nonzebu-presenting stimulation, not only does it activate a disposition to dissent from 'Zebu?', it simultaneously activates a disposition to assent to 'Not one zebu?', and another disposition to assent to 'Not two zebus?', and so on.

Perhaps one need not worry overmuch over the claim that stimulations activate dispositions. Perhaps one could amend it to read, not that stimulations actually activate dispositions, but rather that stimulations would activate dispositions were conditions appropriate. Thus it is true enough that, given present visual stimulation, if a querying linguist were to murmur 'Aardvark?' in my ear, I would, being obliging, respond by dissenting. But since no querying linguist is at my ear, my present nonaardvark-presenting stimulation does not actually activate an 'implicit" disposition to dissent from 'Aardvark?'.

Are stimulations the stuff that significant linguistic correlations are made of? Yes according to Quine, for he fastens only on our nerve endings. In discussing the possible translation of 'Gavagai' as 'Rabbit', he points out that, for his view,

It is important to think of what prompts the native's assent to 'Gavagai?' as stimulations and not rabbits. Stimulation can remain the same though the rabbit be supplanted by a counterfeit. Conversely, stimulation can vary in its power to prompt assent to 'Gavagai' because of variations in angle, lighting, and color contrast, though the rabbit remain the same. In experimentally equating the uses of 'Gavagai' and 'Rabbit' it is stimulations that must be made to match, not animals. (31)

The reasons cited for focusing on stimulations rather than rabbits at once suggest equally good reasons for focusing on, say, the output of the optic nerve to the visual cortex, rather than stimulations. Just as stimulations can remain the same though the rabbit be supplanted, so the output of the optic nerve can remain the same though the stimulation be supplanted; and just as stimulations can be supposed to vary in power to prompt assent though the rabbit remains the same, so the output of the optic nerve can be supposed to vary in power to prompt assent though the stimulation remains the same. The facts that Quine cites as reasons for claiming one must focus on stimulations and not rabbits are nothing more than the differences that can be expected to obtain between proximate and remote causes. Quine claims, however, that ocular irradiations are as close as one can reasonably get:

To look deep into the subject's head would be inappropriate even if feasible, for we want to keep clear of his idiosyncratic neural routings or private history of habit formation. We are after his socially inculcated linguistic usage, hence his responses to conditions normally subject to social assessment. Ocular irradiation *is* intersubjectively checked to some degree by society and linguist alike, by making allowances for the speaker's orientation and the relative disposition of objects. (31)

That it is not feasible at present to look to the visual cortex is true, but would it be inappropriate to do so? Quine says that "we are after" the subject's "socially in-culcated linguistic usage, hence his responses to conditions normally subject to social assessment". His parochial "hence" is revealing: it marks him as the parish Skinner. Yes, we are concerned with the subject's language, with his linguistic usage. What has that to do with responses? Do speakers respond to conditions? as patients to treatment? Quine hopes to construe an informant's overt linguistic behavior as a response to a stimulus. So he supposes that the informant is responding to ocular irradiation. Say, then, that we are concerned with an informant's assents and dissents: these are responses. But these are responses to queries, not to visual stimulations. One can respond to a work of art but it would not be a matter of talking.

The supposition that a stimulation, conceived as a pattern of chromatic irradiation of the eye, "prompts" (to use Quine's preferred word) assent to or dissent from a query is on a par with the supposition that the relevant copulation of Hitler's grandparents "prompted" the outbreak of the Second World War. That visual stimulations can contribute a causal factor influencing assent to or dissent from what is said in uttering some sentences is, however, hardly to be doubted and not here in question. But the causal factors supplied by visual stimulation depend for their efficacy on the functioning of intervening mechanisms not to be accounted for simply in terms of dispositions to assent to or dissent from sentences. The information, so to speak, supplied by the stimulation is processed. There is more to seeing than meets the eye.

The processes involved in perception are appalling in their complexity. A reasonably adequate account is not to be had. But certain features of the processing that takes place can readily be discerned. Processing of stimulation involves some sort of filtration. Attending an association meeting, one turns a deaf ear to the speaker, screening out unwanted stimulation while pretending to be awake. The character of the filtration of auditory stimulation in deep sleep is remarkable: an experienced native will sleep soundly despite rumbling thunder and the screams of hyenas only to be awakened instantly by the soft cough of a prowling linguist.

Possibly some sort of amplificatory system is also in

operation. Despite the deafening din at a cocktail party, if one's name is mentioned across the room, the signal is apt to come in loud and clear. Amplification is apparently a feature of certain phenomena investigated by psychologists: quarters and half dollars look larger to poor children than to rich ones; Harvard yard looks larger to inmates than to visitors; the apparent size of the full moon on the horizon is another case in point.

Apart from filtration and amplification, the processing of stimulation undoubtedly involves remarkably complex operations with storage facilities, so to speak. Certain stimulations are referred to some sort of static storage and either rendered unavailable for processing, or for further processing, or are available only under special conditions. Experiments have shown that subjects under hypnosis, or under appropriate medication, may be capable of correctly reporting details of scenes witnessed which they are otherwise incapable of reporting. Stimulations may also be referred to some sort of dynamic storage and thus rendered immediately available for processing. But in consequence they may be subject to further processing in connection with the processing of other stimulations. Staring out of a window, I see a small animal dash by. What was it? I do not know. Someone asks 'Was that a rabbit?' and on hearing the query I at once reply 'Yes, of course' for of course I then see that it was. Can one ignore all of this? Quine does.

Quine's concept of stimulus meaning has been devised with a view to correlating sentences with stimulations. For altogether explicable reasons, apart from some sentences about stimulations such correlations are of no linguistic significance. That such correlations are of no linguistic significance can be seen by attending to a series of cases.

The stimulus meaning of a sentence for a speaker is the stimulus meaning of that date. As Quine says "we must allow our speaker to change his ways" (33). If a speaker is "prompted once by a given stimulation σ to assent to S, and later, by a recurrence of σ to dissent from S . . . we would simply conclude that his [the speaker's] meaning for S had changed" (33).

Stimulations are not the stuff that significant linguistic correlations are made of. And identifying visual stimulations with patterns of chromatic irradiation of the eye in no way lends color to the proposal. Quine remarks:

In taking visual stimulations as irradiation patterns we invest them with a fineness of detail beyond anything that our linguist can be called upon to check for. But this is all right. He can reasonably conjecture that the native would be prompted to assent to 'Gavagai' by the microscopically same irradiations that would prompt him, the linguist, to assent to 'Rabbit', even though this conjecture rest wholly on samples where irradiations can at best be hazarded merely to be pretty much alike. (31)

Can a linguist reasonably so conjecture? What if the linguist is remarkably myopic, the native excessively presbyopic? Or what if the native has excellent vision, the strabismic linguist forced to wear corrective lenses: should the linguist dispense with glasses to corroborate his conjectures? Is age then bound to effect a linguistic change, for as one ages and eyes fail, there will be a corresponding fluctuation in stimulus meanings: irradiation patterns that once "prompted" assent will cease to do so? Can a defect of the crystalline lens be of linguistic significance? Must linguistics and opthalmology merge?

Consider a native speaker K who is supplied, owing to the efforts of linguist L, with visual stimulation v, where v is a tiger-presenting stimulation. Linguist L queries K at time $t-1$ with 'Tiger?' whereupon K obliging assents. Later at time $t-2$, K is again supplied with v but on hearing L's repeated query 'Tiger?', K, bored with it all, peevishly dissents. Here perhaps one should not, on Quine's account, conclude that the stimulus meaning of 'Tiger' for K has changed, for possibly K's dissent was not "prompted" by stimulation v. (Or so it might be claimed, but when it comes to talk of "prompting", nothing is clear. One could argue that K would not have dissented if, feeling peevish, he had been presented with v and v had proven to be a nontiger—presenting stimulation: in such a case, to manifest his peevishness he would have had to assent.)

Consider then a less peevish case. A neurophysiologist has devised a filter of a sort, to be inserted along the optic nerve, readily insertable and removable, such that if the subject receives a tiger-presenting stimulation, the output of the optic nerve to the visual cortex, once the filter is in place, will be the same as the output of the optic nerve to the visual cortex when no filter is present and the subject receives a nontiger—presenting stimulation. The filter is then tested on K. At time $t-1$, without the filter and supplied with tiger-presenting stimulation v, K assents to the query 'Tiger?'; at time $t-2$, with the filter in place and again supplied with tiger-presenting stimulation v, K dissents from the query 'Tiger?'. The experiment is repeated over and over again, always with the same results. Here it is clear that K's assent and dissent are "prompted" by stimulation v, in so far as any stimulation "prompts" any assent or dissent. It would seem that the filter has been put to a test and that it works. But on Quine's account, the filter has not been tested at all. Since K first assented and then dissented to v, on Quine's account the stimulus meaning of 'Tiger?' for K at time $t-1$ was not the same as at time $t-2$. Furthermore, the stimulus meaning of 'Tiger?' for K must have oscillated throughout the time that the experiment was being repeated.

Perhaps the case is too curious to bother with: when neurophysiologists pry with simian fingers in the fissures of our brains, many of our concepts may totter. Perhaps the concept of stimulus meaning has not been devised with a view to scientific experimentation. But then there are plain cases of a comparable sort.

K and L have learned to converse. On a jungle journey suddenly they come upon a tiger standing on a rock under a banyan tree by a water-hole. L at once queries K: 'Rock?', and K moans 'No you idiot, that's a tiger!'. K had received not simply a rock-presenting stimulation but a tiger-rock-banyan-tree-water-hole-presenting stimulation. On coming face to whisker with a tiger one is not apt to attend to or be concerned with an inconsequential rock. Quine's concept of stimulus meaning runs aground on such a rock as this.

For consider the incessant and, with respect to Quine's conceptual scheme, lugubrious fluctuations in the membership of the class of stimulations that supposedly "prompt" assent to sentences. Suppose the same scene recurs at a later time and during the interval K has come to terms with tigers. Then to the query 'Rock?', K might well respond 'Yes'. Since the stimulation he received was not but now is a member of the class of stimulations that "prompt" assent to 'Rock?', on Quine's account the stimulus meaning of 'Rock?' has changed for K. One can hardly quarrel with an arbitrary stipulation: but what does *K's* former fear of tigers have to do with the meaning, past or present, of the sentence 'Rock?'?

An everyday sort of case: though I am looking right at a pen on my desk, I do not see it amidst all the clutter. In response to the query 'Is there a pen before you?' I say 'No'. A few moments later, suddenly I see it. Then in response to the query repeated I say 'Yes'. Have I suddenly changed the meaning of 'There is a pen before me'? Certainly, given Quine's account of stimulus meaning, the stimulus meaning of the sentence has changed, but that only indicates that the stimulus meaning of a sentence is of no linguistic significance whatever. That I assented to the second query, dissented from the first, is readily explicable in terms of the processing of stimulations and the focusing of attention; there is no need to suppose that any further sort of linguistic change has taken place to account for the switch from 'No' to 'Yes'.

Consider the following sequence of events: a person is told 'Run to the window and see if there is a car in front of the house; it is very important'. Thus he receives auditory stimulation a_1. He then goes to the window, receives visual stimulation v, say one-half second in duration. He returns and is asked 'Is there a cat by the lamp post across the street?'. Thus he receives auditory stimulation a_2. Most likely he will not be able to say. Presumably the reception of a_1 served to effect the processing of v in such a way as to render it unavailable for the processing required to answer the unexpected question.

Since Quine is primarily concerned with cases in which a nonlinguistic stimulation is followed by an auditory stimulation corresponding to a query, he focuses his attention on the ordered pair (v, a_2), thus ignoring the possibility of a_1 and thus would seem to suppose what of course he cannot possibly suppose, either that he is dealing with a *tabula rasa* or that v will be processed in accordance with a_2 prior to the reception of a_2 and regardless of the state of the organism. Suppose the same sequence of events is repeated: the subject is again supplied with stimulation a_1 and then v and then a_2. This time the subject might well respond with either yes or no. Since v was not but now is a member of either the affirmative or negative stimulus meaning of 'Cat by the lamp post across the street?', on Quine's account a change has occurred in the stimulus meaning of that expression for the subject and thus a linguistic change has occurred.

There is no need further to explore the divagations of Quine's paronomastic proxy for meaning. The line between linguistic and nonliguistic change may be only a blur, but that is no reason to blot out the whole spectrum. The instability of stimulus meaning is not indicative of linguistic flux. It is indicative of the utter inutility of that concept for semantic analysis.

Where did things go wrong? There is only one way of being wrong, but there are indefinitely many ways of patching up a theory. I am inclined to fix on two features. First, it is hopeless (or at present hopeless) to attempt a causal account of linguistic behavior. Viable regularities of the form 'If a is the case then a speaker does β' are simply not to be found. (Even Pavlov's dogs defied such descriptions.) One can, however, hope to formulate viable regularities of the form 'If a speaker does β then generally a is the case'. But second, even regularities of that form must initially be taken as only tentative. Such regularities, or what I have elsewhere called "state regularities", must be tested, examined in the framework of analysis for the entire language.[2]

Quine's concept of stimulus meaning is cast in a causal mold; thus it faces the wrong way: it looks from conditions to speakers instead of from speakers to conditions. And it is inflexible. In consequence, it is useless.[3]

[2] *Semantic Analysis* (Ithaca: Cornell University Press, 1960).

[3] I am indebted to Kathryn P. Parsons and Jon Moline for various helpful criticisms.

VII

There's More to Seeing than Meets the Eye

Eyes, light, a conscious observer, an intact visual system, these are what seeing seems to be made of. It seems that if one sees something then that which one sees supplies light to one's eyes. Either by reflection or refraction or emission, that which is seen functions as a source of patterned radiant flux which impinges on the surface of the eyes. The visual system of the conscious observer is then brought into play; the input visual data is subjected to visual processing of some sort with the upshot that the observer sees something. This rough and ready model of what seeing is is, I think, largely right. But there are difficulties, details that are askew. I shall try to attend to one: it isn't exactly true that if one sees something then that which one sees supplies light to one's eyes.

The kind of seeing we are here concerned with calls for eyes, light, a conscious observer with an intact visual system. We are not concerned with the blind. If a blind man can see, that he can hardly alleviates his lot: he can see what the problem is, what is meant, the point; he can also see his dentist, and on occasion he can see that something is the case.

Nor need we more than glance at and pass by a case like 'When I close my eyes I see angels clapping their wings', which is not like seeing pink rats or the like, except that in neither case is there need to speak of that which is seen. Seeing pink rats might well be spoken of as "pink rat seeing" just as hunting unicorns is spoken of as "unicorn hunting": pink rat seeing and unicorn hunting don't require the presence of either unicorns or rats. If one were, which I am not, of a mind to explain all this, one could be concerned to view the at present inaccessible sights along the optic nerve from the eyeball to the visual cortex. Pink rat seeing presumably calls for the activation of stored patterns of light. But what these patterns are, how they are stored, how activated, what with 125,000,000 receptors in each eye to contemplate, are matters I mean to pass by.

On occasion that which one sees perhaps did but does not supply light to one's eyes. This is so when one sees stars that no longer exist as in the sky or on a television late show. What does not exist does not, even if it did, supply light to one's eyes.

What to say about this is far from clear. One could say: why get up tight about matters of tense? Logicians by and large ignore them; narrators often prefer a dramatic present. That which is seen either supplies or supplied light to one's eyes. But I would not applaud such a ploy.

With respect to the stars in the sky that no longer are, I think it is only ignorance that leads literal minded speakers to speak of seeing them. If it were known that the source of the starlight had ceased to exist, would one, even so, claim to see the star? If the star has ceased to exist then, as a matter of fact, one sees not the star but only the starlight.

Seeing Bogart on a television late show is another matter. Literally speaking, one does not: one sees not Bogart but a motion picture of Bogart. To say otherwise is to invite the rejoinder 'You couldn't have seen Bogart last night—he died some years ago'. But that Bogart is dead is likely to be known to those who say 'I saw Bogart last night' and such knowledge suggests that a simple ellipsis is at work here.

Subtler issues issue from the following covey of cases. We are on a dry plain; George climbs into the cab of his truck, waves goodbye, drives down the dusty road, throwing up a cloud of dust in his wake; he is ten miles off, yet we have kept looking and we see George rounding the bend. Looking for a cat in tall grass, one espies the reedy ripple produced by the running cat and cries 'I see the cat'. Catching his shadow cast on a translucent window shade one says 'I see him'. Staring at the blip on a radar screen one says 'I see a submarine'. And so forth.

Did we see George? If pressed, many are inclined to retract: 'I saw a cloud of dust caused by George driving his truck down the dusty road. No, I didn't actually see George'. Just so, many would say not that they did not see but that they did not actually see the cat or the man whose shadow was caught or the submarine. Do we see these things? The right answer seems to be: yes we do see them only we don't actually see them.

The affirmative half of this answer is hard to defend. A principle that more or less fits our covey of cases is this: if by means of his visual input, the patterned radiant flux impinging on the surface of his eyes, an observer locates *c* in his field of vision then the observer sees *c*. The principle fits the case of George ten miles off and that of the cat in tall grass readily, not so easily the others. Catching his shadow cast on a translucent window shade one says 'I see him', but what if the shadow is cast on a wall? Is such a remark then best construed either as untrue or as an ellipsis for 'I see a shadow he casts'? One could sight a shadow cast by a person under conditions in which the person is not locatable within one's field of vision, say the person is above and behind one but in front of a spotlight which casts a shadow on a wall in front of one. If one saw one's own shadow on a wall in front of one, would one see oneself? Spotting the blip on a radar screen one says 'I see a submarine', yet it is the blip and not the submarine that is located in one's field of vision. But then the submarine seems to be sighted as Bogart may be seen on a television late show. Whereas if one points to the blip and says 'That is the submarine' then that which one points to is located in one's field of vision.

No matter how the principle fares in these cases, others give one pause. If you stand with your back to me, I may see your head, which enables me to locate your nose in my field of vision, yet I do not see your nose. Is the difficulty here with the example or the principle? That one is able to locate a nose in his field of vision does not mean that he *does* locate it. But what if one were on a nose hunt and espied the back of a nose bearing head: would he then see a nose? Glimpsing the sunlight glinting on a rifle barrel, one sees the hidden bushwhacker waiting on the hill; one does not see his hands, yet one can locate his hands as well as one can locate him in one's field of vision. If one espies the reedy ripple produced by a cat running in tall grass one sees the cat. One does not see a cat's eye, or even a cat's head.

The cautionary cases cited here all involve parts; but not essentially. Seeing a flea ridden dog walking down the lane, one does not see fleas, yet one can locate fleas in one's visual field by means of the input visual data. It is not parts that matter but relative size. The principle we have been considering appears to be subject to modification by two distinct factors. First, one must face up to the apparent absurdity that little things are used to sight big things, not vice versa. If a car is almost completely buried in sand but one sights a hub cap protruding, one sees the car. But if the hub caps are buried in sand, the car buried up to the wheel tops, and one sights the car, one does not see hub caps. Second, inanimate things are used to sight animate things. If a man with an enormous ball and chain, the ball being larger than the man, is buried in sand with only the ball protruding, if one sights the ball one sees the man. But if the man is protruding, the ball completely buried, if one sights the man one does not see the ball. This last case, perhaps because it flaunts the factor of size, can readily be turned around. Let the ball be of pure platinum, and let the observers be interested in money, not men: then sighting the man protruding they would see the platinum ball.

The insurmountable difficulty in mapping the conception of seeing displayed in the kind of cases we have been considering is that though the cited factors appear to function as relevant parameters, the fundamental factor appears to be the capricious one of interest. For it is easy enough to construct counterexamples in which the big and animate is used to sight the little and inanimate; so a truffle fancier sighting his pig rooting in the ground could well exclaim 'I see a truffle'. Perhaps relative size and animation function as relevant factors largely in virtue of their being indices of interests.

We see George ten miles off, we see the cat running in tall grass, only we don't actually see them. That we don't is not owing simply to the fact that our eye's are not irradiated with light reflected from their bodies. If in Chicago one views, live via satellite, the Wimbledon matches, it is not Laver's powerful arm that supplies light to one's eyes but the glowing TV tube. Just as no light reaches us from George, no light reaches us from the Wimbledon matches seen live on television. Yet the case of Wimbledon is unlike that of George in that yes and only yes is then the right answer to the query 'Do you really see the matches?'.

Is the difference between the cases to be seen in this contrast: looking at Laver at Wimbledon on television and looking at a photograph of Laver in my hand I say 'Yes, that's Laver in the near court'; but standing in the dusty road looking at a photograph of George in my hand, I do not say 'Yes, that's George in the truck'? What I see when I see Laver on TV in some sense or other looks like Laver, whereas what I see when I see George ten miles off does not in the same sense look like George: it looks like a cloud of dust.

There may be something right in or around this account but what is wrong is plain enough. One can see something without knowing that one does and without thereby being enabled to make an identification. If

Josef stands before me with a bag over his head, I will see Josef and perhaps not know that I do. Neither need what I see look like Josef. Of course what I see will, presumably, look like a person and since the person happens to be Josef, I see Josef. But that what I see looks like a person doesn't signify. If Josef were wearing the skin of a gorilla, what I would see would look like a gorilla and yet I would see Josef. Or what if a person contracted and succumbed to a dreadful disfiguring fungus? One might see the person's body even if the body looked not like a body but like a toadstool. If a lady's leg is encased in a cast and I see the cast, do I see her leg? One is, I think, inclined to say this: if the cast is slim and thin and almost skin tight then yes one sees her leg, but if the cast were vast, voluminous, bigger than her body, then no, not really. (Or if yes then yes as in the case of George ten miles off, which is to say yes and no not really.) Why all this is so is not hard to see and not easy to say.

I shall speak of "visual aspects" of cats and men and the moon that one is on occasion presented with.[1] I cannot say precisely what a visual aspect is: it is not a pattern of chromatic irradiation supplied to the eye, neither is it a retinal image. It is rather that which results when such images are subjected to certain processing by seeing beings. Retinal images come early on in the process of visual perception; they are building blocks and not the final edifice: to speak of "visual aspects" is to suggest, albeit vaguely, a culmination of a sort. (To speak of "being presented with a visual aspect" is thus rather like speaking of "baking bread": just as the bread is that which results when one

[1] See my *Philosophic Turnings* (Ithaca: Cornell University Press 1966) ch. iv.

bakes dough, so the visual aspect is that which results upon successful processing of incoming patterned radiant flux.)

If in turning one's eyes toward the full moon one is presented with some visual aspect, the character of that aspect will depend on many factors, on the positions of the moon and of the viewer, the environing conditions and most significantly, for immediate purposes, on a proper subset of the set of physical properties of the moon, on what I shall speak of and refer to as the "visual properties" of the moon. They are those properties of an object in virtue of which the object functions as a source of patterned radiant flux, of patterned electromagnetic waves in the range between infra red and ultra violet. Though one need not be a selenologist to do so, if one is correctly to account for even the grosser features of the presented visual aspect, some relevant reference will have to be made to visual properties of the moon. And only in so far as visual properties of the moon serve to determine features of the presented visual aspect can being presented with such a visual aspect be a case of seeing the moon.

On being presented with a visual aspect supplied by a blip on a radar screen one may say 'I see a submarine'. Yet it is not the case that visual properties of the submarine serve to determine features of the presented visual aspect. On the contrary, features of the presented visual aspect are determined by visual properties of the radar screen and by properties of the submarine in virtue of which the submarine functions as a reflector of ultra high frequency radio waves. Much the same may be said in connection with seeing George ten miles off, the cat running in tall grass, the bushwhacker hidden on the hill: in all such cases, visual properties of that which is seen do not serve to determine features of the presented visual aspects. In contrast, when one sees Laver at Wimbledon on live television via satellite with adequate transmission and reception, features of the presented visual aspect are determined by the image on the TV screen and features of the image on the screen are determined by Laver's visual properties. So features of the visual aspect one is presented with are ultimately determined by Laver's visual properties and so one sees Laver.

It appears to be a *sine qua non* condition for actually seeing something, not that that which one sees supplies light to one's eyes, but that visual properties of that which is seen serve to determine features of the presented visual aspect. As against this, there are common cases of actually seeing something in which this condition appears to be faulted. Looking at a pink girl wearing blue leotards, one may see her legs: only some of the visual properties of her legs, those pertaining to shape but not those pertaining to hue, will serve to determine features of the presented visual aspect: the visual aspect will be that of blue legs.

Legs are like women and not faces. A woman clad from head to foot in a burnoose, her face veiled, the forehead covered, only a slit for the eyes to see, is still to be seen: one sees the woman though not her face. Take a naked woman, cover her from head to foot with a wet clinging sheet: one still sees the woman. Does one see her face? It is not clear but I say no, not exactly. I don't, however, think that much of this has much to do with seeing even though it can look as though it did.

Legs are sometimes bare legs, a woman is often a

woman's body, feet may be bare feet: faces are generally just faces (though no doubt all this depends on the culture and on what turns one on). 'When shall we paint the woman?' on occasion is not significantly different from 'When shall we paint the woman's body?'. But 'Who was that lady I saw you with last night?' does not, except in exceptional circumstances, have anything to do with a lady's body. Josef wearing unmistakable red argyle socks, dogged by a policeman, visiting a foot doctor, whose office has windows to the floor, shades drawn exposing only a slit of light, strips down to his socks, which out of modesty he refuses to doff. Later the dogger testifies that he could see that Josef was in the office for peering through the slit left between shade and floor he could see Josef's feet. The doctor testifies that he never saw Josef's feet since Josef refused to doff his socks. Yet each saw what the other saw. Neither dogger nor doctor saw Josef's bare feet; both saw his stockinged feet.

Cases of seeing legs and the like do not establish that the proposed *sine qua non* condition requires emendation, but it does: on occasion only some of the visual properties of that which is seen serve to determine features of the presented visual aspect. This is so when one sees Laver on a live telecast but in black and white: his visual properties pertaining to hue presumably do not serve to determine features of the presented visual aspect. And does hue matter when figures are seen in a fog? (I am not sure of these matters. But I think that if these cases won't do, others could be found.)

To claim that some of the visual properties of that which is seen serve to determine features of the presented visual aspect is not to claim much. As has been said, they also serve who only stand and wait. Visual properties of that which is seen may participate in the determination of features of the presented visual aspect, but such participation can be altogether minimal and perhaps merely nominal.

Suppose a live telecast of an okapi in an enclosure were shown, but the broadcast signal was subjected to drastic transformation, scrambled in the way wartime radio messages may be scrambled to avoid their being understood by the enemy. Presented with a visual aspect supplied by a thoroughly scrambled image on the TV screen, one would not see the okapi even if features of the presented visual aspect were somehow determined by some of the okapi's visual properties.

Whether one would see the okapi if the TV image were transformed would of course depend both on the character of the transformation and on the visual system of the observer. Any TV image is simply a source of patterned radiant flux. The retinal image, supplied by such flux impinging on the eyes of the observer, requires visual processing if the observer is to be presented with a visual aspect. If a retinal image were the product of certain simple transformations of the patterned radiant flux supplied to the observer, the observer might find that his customary processing of the input data occasioned no great difficulties: the presented visual aspect might be of a kind he could readily cope with. This would be the case for most of us if the retinal image were supplied by a TV image that was slightly bent or curved (in a way a TV image often is with faulty reception). If the retinal image were the product of a more drastic transformation, turned upside down by means of prisms, the difficulty it would occasion an observer would be greater. But as we have all been told, an ordinary observer's visual system is sufficiently flexible to allow changes in the processing of the retinal image; in time, usually after about three months and under appropriate conditions, the visual aspect the observer is presented with, when looking at an okapi and wearing prisms that invert his retinal image, may be virtually identical with the visual aspect he was presented with three months earlier when looking at the same okapi but not wearing the prisms.

If r is a retinal image, P a visual processing that r is subjected to when r is the input data to an observer's visual system, and a is the presented visual aspect, then a can be described as the value of a function P over r. The fact that visual processing is subject to change, as in the inverting prisms case, can then be expressed by saying that there are available to the observer various P's such that given r_i, the observer (in time) finds a P_i such that $P_i(r_i) = a$; given r_j $(j \neq i)$, the observer (in time) finds a P_j such that $P_j(r_j) = a = P_i(r_i)$.

What this indicates, however, is that some visual aspects presented by various things, by okapi and men and the moon, are, in a certain sense, overdetermined. If when confronted with an okapi in an enclosure, thus with a complex, c, one is supplied with retinal image r_i which subjected to processing P_i yields aspect a, and then, owing to the operation of intervening factors serving to transform the patterned radiant flux supplied to the eyes by c, on again confronting complex c one is supplied with retinal image r_j which subjected to processing P_j yields aspect a again, then aspect a would appear to be relatively constant with respect to c. But the constancy of a can hardly be accounted for simply on the basis of c's visual properties. Other factors serve to determine that aspect a be presented.

If r_i yields a when subjected to processing P_i and if r_j is the retinal image that results when the observer wearing inverting prisms is confronted with complex c, then r_j yields b when subjected to processing P_i, where b corresponds to a inverted. In time aspect b is lost, replaced by a when P_i is replaced by P_j. A reason for the caducity of aspect b is not difficult to surmise, though for the time being such a surmise is perhaps devoid of much experimental support. If one is to cope with okapi, catch and play them, feed them, there must be an accommodation between one's perceptual and motor systems. Visual aspects evoke complex responses: the sight of someone falling evokes radically different visceral responses from the sight of someone rising. An inverted visual aspect would of course at once occasion difficulties in the adjustment and coordination of motor responses. Given a complex behavioral system, it may be vastly simpler for an organism to deal with r_j, the inverted retinal image, by changing its method of processing from P_i to P_j so as to yield aspect a, rather than by adhering to P_i which yields b and then making appropriate adjustments elsewhere in the associated perceptual and motor systems.

That there is some sort of overdetermination of visual aspects is indicated not only by cases in which retinal images have been the products of artificial transformations of the kind noted but, more generally, by the well-known constancy phenomena investigated by gestalt psychologists.[2] As Koffka long ago noted, if we are looking at objects

[2] See, for example, Kurt Koffka, *Principles of Gestalt Psychology*, (New York: Harcourt, Brace, 1935) ch. vi.

whose vertical edges project on vertical retinal lines, "as soon as we tilt our heads, vertical lines are no longer projected on vertical retinal lines, and yet the objects which looked vertical before will continue to do so, as long as we are not in a totally dark room in which a vertical luminous line is the only visible object".[3]

Since visual aspects can be readily overdetermined, there may be and probably are cases in which our supposed *sine qua non* condition for actually seeing something is faulted if the condition requires that the service performed by visual properties be more than nominal. Confronted with something *c*, owing to determination by nonvisual factors, one is presented with a visual aspect *a*, which is virtually identical with an aspect of *c* that is presented in cases in which the aspect is significantly determined by visual properties of *c*. Thus suppose that visual aspect *a* has been elicited as a conditioned response to nonvisual cues but in the presence of *c* and in a familiar viewing situation. In such a case, visual properties of *c* serve only in Milton's way.

There is a distinction commonly made between seeing only part or a part of a thing and seeing the thing. If one sees a cat or an apple or a building, there will be part or parts (or segments or bits) of that which one sees that one does not see: these will be internal parts, subvisible parts, molecular parts, parts or the part or a part not facing one, and so forth. Sometimes, with a sensible view to that which one does not see, one says that one sees not the thing but only part of the thing. And sometimes, despite the fact that one does not see what one does not see, one says that one sees not only part but that one sees the thing or one sees the whole thing.

[3] Page 215.

An oryx is in residence at the zoo. On arriving I find that the oryx has withdrawn into a cave, only his left hind hoof is showing. I do not see the oryx: I see only part of the oryx. (Or if one likes, I see but do not actually see the oryx; I see the oryx much as one sees the cat in tall grass.) In the neighboring enclosure, an aoudad stands staring at me through the wire fence. Despite the fact that his rump is not to me, that my view is minimally obscured by the wire fencing, I see the aoudad and not merely only part of the aoudad.

That one sees the aoudad but not the oryx indicates that something is wrong with our proposed *sine qua non* condition for actually seeing something, that some visual properties of that which is seen serve to determine features of the presented visual aspect. In the case of the oryz, not some visual properties of the oryx, but some visual properties of the oryx's left hind hoof serve to determine features of the presented visual aspect. So, in the case of the oryx, our *sine qua non* condition is there faulted with respect to seeing the oryx, but not with respect to seeing the oryx's left hind hoof and thus only part of the oryx. And that is as it should be, or so it may seem. But unfortunately, the condition is also faulted in the case of the aoudad, for again, not some visual properties of the aoudad but some visual properties of only that part of the aoudad that faces one and is not obscured by wire fencing, thus at most some visual properties of, say, the partial forequarter of an aoudad serve to determine features of the presented visual aspect. Since one does see the aoudad, and not only the partial forequarter of the aoudad, our *sine qua non* condition must be emended. It could be etiolated to read: some visual properties of at least part of that which is seen serve to determine features of the presented visual aspect. If all one wants is some *sine qua non* condition or other, possibly this weak one will do. But who will achieve illumination in contemplating it? It will not separate our sheep from our antelope. What is wanted here is an illuminating and yet plausible formulatable statable *sine qua non* condition that accords with a common conception of seeing and that is faulted in the case of the withdrawn oryx, satisfied in the case of the staring aoudad. (That is what is wanted, but I doubt that it is at present to be had for reasons which will appear.)

In the case of the oryx, as in that of the aoudad, features of the presented visual aspect are determined, at least in part, by some visual properties of only part of that which is seen. An easy way of characterizing the difference between the case of the oryx and that of the aoudad is this: though in each case one sees part and not every part of the animal, only in the latter does seeing part constitute seeing the animal. To see part of something is not of course *ipso facto* to see it. To see Madison is not to see Dane County, neither is it to see Wisconsin, or even the Universe. Consider the case of the obliging artist who consents to uncover only one corner of his painting; or that of the man wanting to see the Empire State Building: led up to it blindfolded, unblindfolded with nose to brick, blindfolded again; only a brick, only part, is what he saw. But if seeing part of something sometimes is seeing it, when is it so?

One could look for some sort of probability relation between the seen part and that which it is part of. Perhaps the seen part must be such that there is a high probability that if the part is there to be seen, that which it is part of is too. Will this account for the difference between the oryx and aoudad cases? However one conjures up a probability estimate, it seems that the probability of the oryx being there, given that its left hind hoof is there, would be high indeed, though perhaps less than that of the aoudad being there, given that its forequarter is there. Zoos do not house left hind hooves of oryx without oryx any more than they maintain mounted partial forequarters of aoudads in wire enclosures. Another case: to see someone's open beating heart, exposed for surgery, is not to see the person's body, yet the probability that his body is there given that his beating heart is there is high and maybe as high as the probability in the case of the aoudad.

In lieu of a probability relation, one could look for some sort of representative relation between the part and that of which it is part. Say the seen part must enable an observer to identify that of which it is part. But as against this: to see a woman's elbow is not to see her body yet, as any anthropometrist knows, the elbow of a female humanoid is unmistakable; it is as typical, characteristic and representative a part of a female humanoid body as one could hope to find.

That one sees the aoudad and not the oryx is not to be accounted for in terms of seeing part of something and of when seeing part constitutes seeing that of which it is part. Not parts but patterns, configurations are what matter here. Consider a small dull jet black creature seen in a green field. One sees part but not every part of the creature and yet not only part for one sees the creature. This would seem to be a case in which seeing the part constitutes seeing the creature. If one sees the part then some visual properties of that part serve to determine certain features of one's retinal image and hence serve to determine features of the presented visual aspect. The field then changes from green to dull jet black and of precisely the right quality to render the small creature invisible. One no longer sees the creature, yet the same part of the creature makes the same contribution to the determination of one's retinal image. Or consider someone taking a one-eyed look at an incomplete circle but in such a way that the blind spot of the eye is fixed on the small absent arc that would complete the circle. He does not see the incomplete circle for it is lost in what he does see: the presented visual aspect is that of a complete circle. Suppose he shifts his eye so that the blind spot is no longer fixed on the absent arc. He then sees the incomplete circle and yet the same part was seen in each case.

Why is it that one sees the aoudad but not the oryx, only part of the oryx? The right answer is too hard and too easy: one does not see the oryx because the presented visual aspect lacks the requisite qualities for being an instance of seeing an oryx rather than an instance of seeing only part of an oryx; and in the case of seeing the aoudad the presented visual aspect does not lack the requisite qualities for being an instance of seeing an aoudad.

Visual aspects have staggeringly many and complex qualities. But I cannot tell you precisely what they are. I don't know that. But you and I generally do know when an aspect does and when it does not have the requisite qualities to be an instance of seeing a particular thing. There are, however, certain obvious things to say.

If one sees only the left hind hoof of the oryx, the presented visual aspect is what I shall call "a small-part-of-an-animal-aspect". It is a small-part-of-an-animal-aspect not because of its provenance but because of its character and its qualities. If the oryx has withdrawn into his cave with only the left hind hoof showing, one's visual aspect is a part-aspect perhaps because of the factor of overlap: the figure of the hoof in the presented aspect is overlapped by the figure of the cave side. What makes the aspect a part-of-an-animal-aspect is much less clear. Perhaps that is determined by factors pertaining to shape, and perhaps by factors pertaining to texture, contrasts between figure and ground, and so on. What makes the aspect a small-part-of-an-animal-aspect must be enormously complicated: sharpness of contours, location in the visual field, stereoscopic depth, these are only some of the relevant interrelated factors.

How many relevant factors are there? How many distinct qualities can visual aspects have? How many distinct visual aspects can be presented? Von Neumann, concerned with similar questions with visual analogies, with the fact that one can recognize all sorts of figures as triangular in appearance, conjectured:

About one fifth of the brain is a visual brain, which, as far as we know, does nothing except make decisions about visual analogies. So, using the figures we have, which are not very good, but which are probably all right for an orientation, we conclude that apparently a network of about 2 billion relays does nothing but determine how to organize a visual picture. It is absolutely not clear a priori that there is any simpler description of what constitutes a visual analogy than a description of the visual brain.[4]

[4] *Theory of Self-Reproducing Automata* (Urbana and London: University of Illinois Press, 1966) 47.

It isn't true that if one sees something then that which one sees supplies light to one's eyes. It is true that if one sees something then some visual properties of at least part of that which is seen serve to determine features of the presented visual aspect and the visual aspect has certain qualities requisite for the presentation of the aspect to be an instance of seeing that which is seen. And though this is a remarkably vague conclusion, there is nothing for it. Psychologists and particularly gestalt psychologists have made a beginning. But the morphology of visual aspects has not yet been described. Perhaps it never will be.[5]

[5] I am indebted to A. Phillips Griffiths, to Rita Nolan, and to Eva Aoudad for many helpful suggestions and criticisms.

VIII

Something about Conceptual Schemes

Despite tiresome explications ununderstanding may be rife and rampant. A fulsome detailing of particulars may aggravate without alleviating a failure of communication. Contrariwise, a choice grimace can sometimes suffice to convey even a subtle suggestion. Not prolixity however but an aspect of the etiology of ununderstanding is our immediate concern.

The causes of ununderstanding are legion: any factor relevant to the understanding of what is said may contribute equally to an instance of ununderstanding. Thus phonetic, phonemic, morphologic, syntactic, semantic, discourse and perceptual factors may be operative, may effect a lack or a failure of understanding or even a misunderstanding of what is said. But what I am principally concerned with here are what I shall call "specifications" or, more precisely, "an absence of specifications".

I have in mind certain careless cases: in them communication proceeds succeeds readily easily; no one notices anything out of the ordinary, for nothing is, and no one seems to wonder. A case: a cheetah is a fast feline; such is the common conception, mine too; cheetahs have been clocked at eighty miles an hour; one says then 'A cheetah can outrun a man'. And is one apt to be understood? Of course! But how and why are hard to say or even see.

There are cases of ununderstanding mediated by the use of special words but this is not apt to be one of them. Had one said 'A zibet can outrun a man' some would wonder: 'zibet' is perhaps a rare name for a common civet cat. 'Cheetah' is a known name of a common sort of cat.

Standards criteria and the like sometimes give one pause, occasion genuine ununderstanding. 'Have you been in Kalamazoo?'. I cannot cope with that query without wagging the following tale: 'I was on a train that rolled slowly through Kalamazoo; I looked through the window; I did not get off: have I been in Kalamazoo?'. That is not the way it is with cheetahs outrunning men.

Where words and standards are plain and easy, grammar or syntax or cooccurrence conundrums may still cause one to come a cropper: 'I couldn't fail to disagree with you less' said the late President Eisenhower tripping a fine linguistic trap. The syntax of 'A cheetah can outrun a man' is as standard as can be.

One says 'A cheetah can outrun a man'. We put it to a test: a man and a cheetah are turned loose in a field. The man lopes away while the cheetah sits lazily in the sun. But 'can' is not 'will'. The cheetah can even if it did not. We try again. This time we force the cheetah to run by beating it; but the man easily outruns the cheetah: the cat encumbered with an awkward two-hundred-pound weight moves slugggishly.

An encumbered cheetah is a cheetah. And I said a cheetah can outrun a man. Should I have said not that a cheetah can but, more cautiously, that some cheetahs can outrun a man, namely unencumbered cheetahs? But what about an unencumbered cheetah whose feet have been bound since birth? If we make provision for foot-bound unencumbered cheetahs shall we not also have to provide a place for three-legged cheetahs, drugged cheetahs, cheetahs forced to run after being force fed and so on and on? Would it be better then simply to say 'Some—never mind which—cheetahs can outrun a man'?

But communication gropes stumbles and eventually collapses when the forthright 'A cheetah can outrun a man' is so cautiously qualified. It is true that some—never mind which—cheetahs can outrun a man. But it is also true that some—never mind which—men can outrun a cheetah (namely those able ones racing against disabled cheetahs). And it is also true that some—never mind which—cheetahs cannot outrun a man and some—never mind which—men cannot outrun a cheetah. So so far men and cheetahs would seem to be on a par with respect to running. But they are not: a cheetah can outrun a man. Another case: cheetahs don't have horns; what about a cheetah that has been subjected to a successful horn graft? Should we conclude that then anyway some cheetahs don't have horns? Possibly some feel a temptation to switch from 'a cheetah' to 'some cheetahs' when they ponder the remark 'A cheetah can outrun a man'. But not many are likely to feel such a temptation when pondering the remark 'Cheetahs don't have horns'.

These cheetah cases are not curious special or rare. Similar problems are encountered when one considers and ponders such comments as 'A tiger is a large carnivore': isn't a. new-born tiger a tiger and yet hardly a large carnivore? 'Skim milk is a healthful food': isn't skim milk laced liberally with strychnine nonetheless skim milk and hardly healthful? 'This car gets thirty-five miles to the gallon': what about the leak in the fuel tank?

In each of these cases a difficulty lies lurking in an absence of specifications. One says 'A cheetah' and no further specification of what one is speaking of is given; one says simply 'A tiger', 'Skim milk', 'This car'. And as comments could occasion confusion, so could commands and queries. There is, indeed, no lack of a variety of cases exemplifying an evident absence of specifications, cases in which, though a possible ununderstanding lies lurking, communication usually proceeds smoothly and easily and free of difficulty.

An officer to a private: 'Shut the door!'. 'Sir' says the private and does nothing else. 'Shut the door!' is not the same as 'Shut the door now!'. 'Shut the door now!' said a wily officer whereupon a wilier private responded with 'Sir' at once shutting and immediately reopening the door. 'Shut the door now!' is not the same as 'Shut the door now and leave it shut!'. 'Open the door!' said an officer but a private refused on the grounds that the preceding year the officer's superior had said to him 'Shut the door and leave it shut!' and that order had not been rescinded.

Another case: students are enjoined not to leave a classroom while a lecturer is there lecturing, and this on pain of expulsion. What if a fire breaks out in the classroom during a lecture: is a student forced to choose between flames and expulsion? In the interests of sanity we could accordingly modify the explicit formulation of the rule to read 'Students are not to leave a classroom while a lecturer is there lecturing unless a fire breaks out'. But if students need not face fire, must they confront an invasion of soldier ants, stay for a saber-toothed tiger, ignore a sudden infestation of cobras? Or what if a student requires an immediate appendectomy? Or what if a student is heavy bored?

Another case: What time is it? Where? Here of course. When? Now! According to what standard? What time is it here and now according to Eastern Standard time? But when? When the question was first raised or now? And does that mean when I am done or when you last closed your mouth? With what degree of precision? Plus or minus ten hours? And anyway, according to whose timepiece?

One says 'A cheetah can outrun a man' and one says simply 'A cheetah': further specifications of what one is speaking of are usually not given, usually not wanted. Is it simply that further specifications are in fact implicit in the discourse? But can't what is implicit in discourse be made explicit? Yet when one attempts to detail, to enumerate some set of specifications that would serve to safeguard the truth of a remark like 'A cheetah can outrun a man', the task seems impossible. It is not merely that such a set of specifications would have to have indefinitely many and anyway prodigiously many members but its membership would have to be remarkably heterogeneous. If there were any such set it seems that its vastness and heterogeneity would preclude the possibility of an effective specification of its membership.

A familiar compendious way of coping with cases requiring some specification is by means of an appeal to what is normal or to what is ordinary or common or typical or standard or characteristic and so forth. So one says 'A cat has four legs, a tail, whiskers, at least ordinary ones do'. An appeal to what is ordinary would seem to provide a sufficient specification to safeguard a remark like 'Cheetahs don't have horns'. The query 'What about a cheetah that has undergone a successful horn graft?' can then readily be replied to with 'Ordinary cheetahs don't have horns'.

But what is supposed to count as an "ordinary cheetah"? How many spots does an "ordinary cheetah" have? Can it growl? Can it growl for an hour? a week? a year? Can it whistle "Dixie"? How old is an "ordinary cheetah"? A specification in terms of what is "ordinary" is not apt to be illuminating if what is "ordinary" is itself so singularly difficult to specify.

An appeal to what is ordinary or normal and so forth seems to constitute an adequate safeguarding specification in some cases, partially so in others, and not at all in still others. Thus the commment 'Ordinary cheetahs don't have horns' seems to be true as it stands, is in no need of further specification. 'A tiger is a large carnivore' is only partially firmed up by the specification 'A normal tiger is a large carnivore' for of course adulthood is a further relevant factor. Thus the comment 'A normal adult tiger is a large carnivore' seems to be true as it stands, is in no need of further specification. (But what if there were a machine, a tiger-shrinking device, available such that a normal adult tiger could be shrunk to the size of a newborn tiger? Then I suppose a further specification could be required here. One could say 'A normal unshrunken adult tiger is a large carnivore'. Since no such device exists, no such specification is required.)

An appeal to what is ordinary or normal and so forth accomplishes nothing at all in connection with the comment 'A cheetah can outrun a man'. The comment 'A normal cheetah can under normal conditions outrun a normal man' is merely obscure. Cheetahs don't ordinarily typically commonly or even normally race against men or for that matter against anything. They do chase after and catch antelopes. What are the normal conditions under which a normal cheetah can outrun a normal man? Is the terrain to be rough or smooth? Say it doesn't matter, that either rough or smooth is to count as normal. Then what if the lay of the land is such that it is slow rough broken uneven under the cheetah's feet, flat fast and easy beneath the man's feet? Are these to count as normal conditions? An appeal to normality is bound to be futile when it consists in nothing more than the invocation of a label. Again, normality would appear to be irrelevant in connection with the comment 'This car gets thirty-five miles to the gallon'. The vehicle in question might be used for commuting from Long Island to New York and thus typically operated in traffic jams. The relevant specification in this sort of case would require an appeal to optimum operating conditions and to some sort of ideal road conditions under which the vehicle is envisaged as being operated.

In the case of commands injunctions and the like, in place of an otiose appeal to what is normal or typical or common or ordinary, one might hope to formulate some sensible principles with which to parry any thrust arising from an absence of specifications. Thus one might contend that to understand a command is to understand that the command is to be obeyed, that the action that constitutes performance of the command is to be performed, as soon as is feasible. So if one is told to shut a door and there is a door at hand to shut then one is to shut the door at once. Whereas if one is told in the middle of the night to eat three meals a day, one can comply by waiting till breakfast time and beginning then. The view in question would thus be that implicit in explicit injunctions is the enjoinder 'Perform as soon as is feasible!'.

The supposition that there is such an implicit enjoinder

is plausible in a few cases, implausible in many. Explicit negative injunctions resist it. 'Don't eat meat!': there is no action that constitutes performance; in consequence one can hardly perform as soon as is feasible. And can one seriously suppose that there is an enjoinder to perform as soon as is feasible implicit in such injunctions as 'Stay awake!', 'Exercise self-restraint!', 'Keep off the grass!'?

Even if one could somehow sensibly suppose that, despite the evident difficulties, implicit to many explicit injunctions is an enjoinder to perform as soon as is feasible, our problems here are scarcely less troublesome than they were: one would still have to invoke still other implicit factors with which to fend off the folly that may be found in the absence of specifications. Thus one would have to conceive of some sort of principle to the effect that one is not to undo what one has done, some principle that would serve to block the move by which, say, after complying with the command to shut a door, one immediately reopened it. And if one succeeded in conceiving of and formulating such a principle, still further principles would be needed to cope with still other absurdities that may abound in the absence of specifications. In short, the difficulties inherent in any attempt to furnish some safeguarding set of specifications are equally to be found in any attempt to furnish some safeguarding set of principles.

Appeals to normality and to principles do little to resolve the issues posed by an absence of specifications; appeals to reasonableness, though perhaps self-satisfying, are equally inefficacious. Thus in the case of the rule to the effect that students are not to leave a classroom while a lecturer is there lecturing, instead of attempting to state an unstatable list of exceptions and escape clauses, one could append to the explicit formulation of the rule the clause 'unless there is good and sufficient reason to do so'. And would that make anything clearer? When is there good and sufficient reason to do so and when not? When a fire breaks out, or when there is an invasion of soldier ants, and so on. But the problem still is: how on?

I say 'A cheetah can outrun a man' but what about a cheetah encumbered with an awkward two-hundred-pound weight? It can't outrun a man. Then it is untrue that a cheetah can outrun a man? No. It is true that an encumbered cheetah is a cheetah, and it is also perhaps true that an encumbered cheetah cannot outrun a man. But it does not follow that a cheetah cannot outrun a man. When I say 'A cheetah can outrun a man' am I speaking of an unencumbered cheetah or of an encumbered cheetah? Neither.

If one meets a cheetah on his way then either one meets an unencumbered cheetah or one meets an encumbered cheetah. Either he had a chicken in his mouth or he did not. (When it comes to cheetahs in a henhouse, there is no *tertium quid*: the principle of excluded middle rules the roost.) But one can speak of a cheetah and think about a cheetah that is neither unencumbered nor encumbered.

A cheetah can outrun a man: any cheetah? No. Then only some? No, not that either. A cheetah that can outrun a man is like Hamlet and like Macbeth. Did Hamlet have an aunt? Was Macbeth's left foot larger than his right? These questions go unanswered: there are no answers to give. When I said 'A cheetah can outrun a man' did I mean a cheetah with long white whiskers or one without long white whiskers? Neither one nor the other. But there is no such thing as a real live cheetah that is neither one nor the other. But that only means that if one points at a real live cheetah then one is pointing either at a cheetah with long white whiskers or at a cheetah without long white whiskers. And that is all right here because speaking of a cheetah and pointing at a real live cheetah need not be the same in this respect.

Speaking of a cheetah, as one does when one says 'A cheetah can outrun a man', is like modeling a cheetah in clay or like doing a pictorial representation of a cheetah. Staring at a pictorial representation of a man in ordinary black opaque unbulgy riding boots we need not ask: is that man a web-footed or a nonweb-footed fellow? A real live man must be one or the other, but a man in a picture is not a real live one.[1]

One has a conception of a cheetah: a long-legged spotted cat, about the size of a small leopard, and having blunt nonretractile claws. And one has a conception of a man, and a conception of running, and of outrunning, and of what can or cannot be and so forth. One's different conceptions of these different matters are related and interrelated in diverse ways; they form what may be called "a conceptual scheme".

I say 'A cheetah can outrun a man': in so doing I indicate that my conception of a cheetah, of running, of outrunning, of a man and so forth all stand in certain specific relations. It is as though a cheetah, a man, running, outrunning and what can be are all different points in some conceptual field: in telling a hearer that a cheetah can outrun a man I offer him, as it were, a bit of a map of a portion of that field indicating certain relations between the indicated points.

[1] See my *Philosophic Turnings* (Ithaca: Cornell University Press, 1966) ch. iv.

But if he is to understand what is said then it is up to him to read the map aright. As the woman Crookback says in the *Chuang Tzu:* "It is easier to explain the Way of a sage to someone who has the talent of a sage, you know".

If the hearer is to understand what is said then the hearer, like the speaker, must have some sort of conceptual scheme; he must have some conception of a cheetah, and of a man, of running and so forth. If he conceives of a cheetah as being about the size of a small leopard and as being a long-legged spotted cat and so forth and if his conceptual scheme is of a common kind and his beliefs of a familiar sort and so forth then if thoughts of absent specifications come to plague him in connection with the comment that a cheetah can outrun a man, he will be able to give them the treatment they deserve. For he will see that to say that a cheetah can outrun a man is not to say anything about whiskered or unwhiskered cheetahs. For whether or not a cheetah has whiskers makes no difference at all when what is in question is running ability. Neither is it to say anything significant about encumbered or unencumbered cheetahs. If a cheetah can outrun a man then so can an unencumbered cheetah; whereas if an encumbered cheetah cannot outrun a man that only shows what one knew all along, that an encumbrance is an encumbrance. For he will himself be able to figure out that an animal about the size of a small leopard encumbered with an awkward two-hundred-pound weight would be hard put to outrun a man. And in like vein without exercising excessive ingenuity he should also be able to figure out for himself that the existence of dead cheetahs has no relevant bearing on the truth of the claim that a cheetah can outrun a man.

If a hearer is to understand what is said then not only must the hearer, like the speaker, have some sort of conceptual scheme but he must also understand the form of representation employed by the speaker when the speaker says 'A cheetah can outrun a man'. Cheetahs, ordinary real live cheetahs, have been clocked running at eighty miles an hour. No man has ever run at that speed. Reflecting on these truths and incorporating these statements in one's conceptual scheme may lead one to the related truth that a cheetah can outrun a man. And presumably the speaker in claiming that a cheetah can outrun a man had in mind as exemplars those ordinary real live cheetahs that were clocked running at eighty miles an hour.

But there is of course no necessity here to adopt just that form of representation, to fix on such exemplars. For one's focus could readily be different. Reflecting not on the truths indicated but on other matters, one could state what would seem to be a contradictory view. For suppose it were the case that though we were interested in comparing the running abilities of men and cheetahs, only aged and infirm cheetahs were of interest to us. Assuming that aged and infirm cheetahs tend to be slow and reflecting on these matters and incorporating the appropriate statements in one's conceptual scheme, one could easily be led to incorporate the related truth that a cheetah cannot outrun a man. Another case: a tiger is a large carnivore. What about a newborn tiger? We focus on the adult of the species. We adopt a particular form of representation, a particular form of projection, much as in map making we might, in a particular case to serve our particular needs, prefer a Mercator projection. But we could, were there reason to do so, alter our focus, adopt a different form of projection:

a tiger is a small carnivore, for a newborn tiger is small. But then of course what about an adult tiger? No picture captures everything: even the best picture of a cat won't purr.

Focusing and a shifting of focus is readily seen in connection with contrafactuals. For on the assumption that the antecedent of the contrafactual is true, that is, if such-and-such were true, one concludes that the consequent would be true. But the character and truth of the consequent depend on the conceptual scheme in which the antecedent statement is assumed to be incorporated and on the measures taken to accommodate the truth of the antecedent. One says 'If Caesar were in Viet Nam now, he'd drop the hydrogen bomb'. But shifting focus one could just as well claim 'If Caesar were in Viet Nam now, he'd use catapults'. I say 'If I were in New York now then I wouldn't be in Canada. But I could also say 'If I were in New York now then I'd be in London and New York at the same time'.

How far can one go here? Could one claim and truly that cheetahs have horns? It is certainly true that cheetahs don't have horns. But is there a shift of focus, a change of one's point of view and a different, a novel, form of representation that would warrant the claim that cheetahs have horns? I don't think that at present there is but I don't see why there couldn't be. For suppose we were cornuphiles and had found a way to give a cheetah horns and suppose we were interested in devolping a race of horned cheetahs. These cheetahs yet to be could be our exemplars, could set the standards in terms of which cheetahs are to be characterized. So one perhaps could then say 'A cheetah would be a difficult pet' without supplying or requiring the specification 'horned'; and perhaps one could then say 'People tend to disdain hornless cheetahs'. And one could say 'A cheetah is a horned spotted long-legged cat' and to the query 'What about all the cheetahs to be seen today?' one could reply 'Only inferior hornless cheetahs are to be found at the moment'.

If a hearer is to understand what is said then he must have some sort of conceptual scheme and he must understand and appreciate the form of representation employed by the speaker. How he understands the latter is, I must confess, largely a mystery to me, at least at present. I suspect it will continue to be so for some time. Possibily it has something to do with the fact that a truly understanding hearer is likely to be a speaker as well; possibly for the most part a hearer is apt to assume that a speaker employs the same form of representation as he, the hearer, would were he to be the speaker. Sometimes of course a switch in a form of representation is altogether apparent. Thus *Webster's Seventh New Collegiate Dictionary* writes after 'alpenstock': "a long iron-pointed staff used in mountain climbing". After 'palimpsest' it writes: "writing material (as a parchment or tablet) used two or three times after earlier writing has been erased". One could have a new alpenstock, one that had never been used, but one could not have a palimpsest that had never been used, or at least an unused parchment could not be a palimpsest. Again, after 'doorplate' it is written: "a nameplate on a door". And after 'headache' it is written: "pain in the head". But if a nameplate were removed from the door and put on a shelf it would still be a doorplate. But a headache isn't a headache unless it's in the head: even if the pain or ache began in the head and seemed to shift downwards to one's left ankle, one wouldn't have a headache in one's ankle.

When it comes to understanding commands injunctions and so forth it seems plausible to suppose that the hearer takes the speaker to be employing a form of representation such that exemplars of whatever it is that constitutes compliance with the command are to be found in the hearer's experience. Thus if a hearer is told 'Shut the door!' it is as though he were told 'Do that which is done such that when it is done you will have obeyed the command "Shut the door!"!'. And if that were so then in a familiar case there would be no question of now or later, of shutting and immediately reopening the door; for such questions do not ordinarily arise, are not likely to arise if one does do that which is ordinarily done.

One speaks and hopes to be understood. Perhaps there is some satisfaction to be found in the fact that both speakers and hearers can contribute their fair share to instances of ununderstanding. At any rate, despite an avid desire to achieve true niggardliness in this respect, I dare say that I have done more than my bit here.

Bibliography
(of works referred to)

Church, Alonzo. *Introduction to Mathematical Logic*. Princeton: Princeton University Press, 1956.

——. Review, The Journal of Symbolic Logic, V (1940).

Cohen, Paul. *Set Theory and the Continuum Hypothesis*. New York: W. A. Benjamin, 1966.

Empson, William. *The Structure of Complex Words*. New York: New Directions, n.d.

Goodman, Nelson. *The Structure of Appearance*. Cambridge: Harvard University Press, 1951.

Grice, H. P. "Meaning," *The Philosophical Review*, LXVI (1957), 377–388.

Koffka, Kurt. *Principles of Gestalt Psychology*. New York: Harcourt, Brace, 1935.

Neumann, John von. "Probabilistic Logics and the Synthesis of Reliable Organisms from unreliable Components." In C. E. Shannon and J. McCarthy, eds., *Automata Studies*. Princeton: Princeton University Press, 1956, 43–98.

——. *Theory of Self-Reproducing Automata*. Urbana and London: University of Illinois Press, 1966.

Quine, W. V. O. *Mathematical Logic*. New York: Norton, 1940.

——. "On Universals," *The Journal of Symbolic Logic*, XII (1947), 75.

——. *Word and Object*. Cambridge Technology Press, 1960.

Reichenbach, Hans. *Elements of Symbolic Logic*. New York: Macmillan, 1947.

Sibley, Frank, and Paul Ziff. *O Bitter Dicta*. Beirut: Punitive Press, 1960.

Tarski, Alfred. *Introduction to Logic*. New York: Oxford University Press, 1941.

Whorf, Benjamin L. *Language, Thought, and Reality*. Cambridge: Technology Press, 1956.

Ziff Paul. *Philosophic Turnings*. Ithaca: Cornell University Press, 1966.

——. *Semantic Analysis*. Ithaca: Cornell University Press, 1960.

Index

Understanding Understanding

Designed by R. E. Rosenbaum.
Composed by Vail-Ballou Press, Inc.,
in 11 point linotype Electra, 3 points leaded,
with display lines in monotype Deepdene.
Printed letterpress from type by Vail-Ballou Press
on Warren's No. 66 text, 60 pound basis,
with the Cornell University Press watermark.
Bound by Vail-Ballou Press
in Columbia book cloth
and stamped in All Purpose foil.

Library of Congress Cataloging in Publication Data
(For library cataloging purposes only)

Ziff, Paul, date.
  Understanding understanding.

  Bibliography: p.
    1. Comprehension.   2. Languages—Psychology.
I. Title.
BF325.Z53   410'.1   72-4573
ISBN 0-8014-0744-3